New Testament Writers and the Old Testament

John M. Court has taught Theology and Religious Studies at the University of Kent for over thirty years, for much of that time as head of department. He edited the New Testament Readings series (Routledge) and collaborated with his wife to write *The New Testament World* (Cambridge University Press/Prentice-Hall, 1990). His particular interest is in the Book of Revelation, on which he has published for SPCK and Sheffield Academic Press.

New Testament Writers and the Old Testament

An Introduction

Edited by

JOHN M. COURT

WIPF & STOCK · Eugene, Oregon

Wipf and Stock Publishers
199 W 8th Ave, Suite 3
Eugene, OR 97401

New Testament Writers and the Old Testament
An Introduction
By Court, John M.
Copyright©2002 by Court, John M.
ISBN 13: 978-1-61097-048-8
Publication date 1/25/2011
Previously published by SPCK, 2002

"'Who Has Believed Our Message?' Paul's Reading of Isaiah"
was previously published in Richard B. Hays, The Conversion
of the Imagination: Paul as Interpreter of Israel's Scripture
(Grand Rapids: Eerdmans, 2005), pp. 25-49.

Contents

	Contributors	vii
1	Introduction	1
2	The Birth of Jesus Christ According to Matthew and Luke	13
3	The Old Testament in the Book of Revelation: A Review of Two Books by G. K. Beale	26
4	Old Testament Quotations in the Gospel of John *Maarten J. J. Menken*	29
5	'Who has believed our message?': Paul's Reading of Isaiah *Richard B. Hays*	46
6	Paul, Scripture and Ethics *Christopher Tuckett*	71
	Index of Old Testament Quotations in New Testament Passages	98
	Index of New Testament Passages containing Old Testament Quotations	113
	Select Bibliography	128
	Index	131

Contributors

Richard B. Hays is the George Washington Ivey Professor of New Testament at the Divinity School, Duke University (Durham, North Carolina, USA). His scholarly work has bridged the disciplines of biblical criticism and literary studies and has explored the innovative ways in which early Christian writers interpreted Israel's scripture. Professor Hays is the author of six books, including *Echoes of Scripture in the Letters of Paul* (Yale University Press, 1989). A collection of his essays on the interpretation of the Old Testament in the New is scheduled for publication in 2003 under the title *The Conversion of the Imagination* (Eerdmans).

Dr Maarten J. J. Menken, author of *Old Testament Quotations in the Fourth Gospel* (Peeters, 1996), is Professor of New Testament Exegesis at the Catholic Theological University, Utrecht, The Netherlands. He specializes in the early Christian use of the Old Testament.

Christopher Tuckett is Professor of New Testament Studies at the University of Oxford. He is the author of a number of books, including, most recently, *Q and the History of Early Christianity* (T & T Clark, 1997) and *Christology and the New Testament* (Edinburgh University Press, 2001). He has also written scholarly essays and articles.

1

Introduction

Most modern translations of the Bible no longer include cross-references in the margin to indicate the sources of Old Testament quotations (or allusions) in the New Testament writings. As a result students using the New Testament, for example the regular edition of the New Revised Standard Version, find it difficult to appreciate the extent of Old Testament reference in the New Testament, let alone make an estimate of the relative weighting of Old Testament themes in different New Testament writings. What is offered in the present volume is primarily a student textbook or resource to deal with this problem, but of course it is equally useful to church study groups or the general reader, not least when considering the appropriateness of major themes in Biblical Theology from the twentieth century, such as 'Promise and Fulfilment'. Such a resource can be further justified on the grounds that the issue of how the Old Testament is used in the New Testament is currently a matter of fierce debate among scholars who argue about the extent to which early Christians in the first century CE would have acknowledged the Hebrew Bible as scripture, and whether they as writers and readers/hearers would have known it by heart. In these ways the presuppositions and methods of the use of the Old Testament in the New Testament world are today once again a centre of controversy.

New Testament Christianity in Relation to the Jewish Scriptures

The subject matter of this volume is what Francis Watson described as 'the Christian Old Testament, distinct from the New Testament but inseparable from it and shaping the way that it is used, as well as being reciprocally shaped by it'.[1] The intertextuality or relationship between these texts constitutes the basic data of this volume, but its significance extends much further, to the definition of the early Christian community and the formulation of Christian doctrine. Christianity is unique among world religions in being born with a ready-made Scripture, a Bible in its cradle. This was the Bible that Christians inherited from Judaism, and it seems that they acknowledged its authority unquestioningly – although, towards the end of the second century CE, they started to refer to it, with critical implications, as the '*Old* Testament'. The exact limits of the contents of the Old Testament may well not have been finally fixed by the start of the New Testament period, but there was already sufficient clarity of definition for the books to be referred to collectively as 'scripture' or 'the scriptures', or by an initial reference to their tripartite structure as 'the law of Moses, and the prophets, and the psalms' (Luke 24.44).[2]

The effects of this scripture on the first Christians were far-reaching. For most of them it was their only literature; and, partly because it was the Bible Jesus used, it was their principal frame of reference. Inevitably it evoked and directed their religious thinking, as an authoritative work by which the religious issues of the day could be decided. For some at least of the early Christians, Biblical study (the reading and interpreting of the Old Testament) was an essential activity. It was claimed that the good news of Jesus was 'in accordance with the scriptures', or, what amounts to the same thing, that it was 'according to the plan and foreknowledge of God'. To understand the Old Testament a wide range of interpretations were available within Judaism: there were the expositions of the rabbis as well as a variety of interpretations from sectarian groups such as that at Qumran, with its library of Dead Sea Scrolls.

But for the Christians their new faith was not necessarily a straightforward continuation of the Jewish past. There were certain features of the tradition which grew up within Christianity itself that gave rise to new approaches to the Old Testament, fresh ways of handling and interpreting it. For example, there was criticism of the Pharisees, and of the interpretation of some of the Old Testament laws, reflected in certain quarters from the teaching which Jesus had given. And an apparently hot-tempered man called Paul had expressed himself forcibly, to the Galatian church in particular, about what was wrong with the Jewish Law, and with the way the 'foolish Galatians' harked back to it. Furthermore, the major period in Judaism for interpreting the Law had begun when the voice of spontaneous prophecy had died out in Israel. Now, with the birth of the Christian movement, there was a rebirth of inspired prophetic activity, and this could not be ignored.

INTRODUCTION

However much the Jewish Bible was esteemed by Christian groups, there was a detectable shift in the centre of gravity. Christianity claimed to be not simply a 'religion of the Book' (literally 'the word'), but the religion of Christ, who was alive through resurrection (and could be called the personal Word of God). While for the Jewish leaders scripture was essentially a matter of Torah (Law), for Christian interpreters scripture was essentially prophecy. This meant that Christians placed the primary emphasis on the second rather than the first section of the Hebrew Bible. For the rabbinic teachers of Judaism scripture was instruction in the way of life that was willed for man by God. In the hands of Christian interpreters, scripture was treated as a quarry for predictions which found their fulfilment in Christ and his Church. It is hardly surprising that the Christians upset the rabbis: both were making use of material from the same Bible, but the Christians were defying established priorities, and insisting on using their own (sectarian) methods of interpretation, while rejecting the traditional methods and procedures of the rabbis. A traditional Christian who has tried to debate with Jehovah's Witnesses on the doorstep about the meaning of scripture might well sympathize with the rabbis.

It was a fact, however, that Jesus himself had used and interpreted the Old Testament as scripture. And with a ready-made authoritative work of scripture in existence, the product of so many generations of Israel, this naturally had the effect of inhibiting any thought of producing new books of scripture, if and when this thought occurred. Although the early Christians were sure they had vitally important 'good news' about Jesus to proclaim, there is more than a suggestion of reluctance in the early Church to write it down. Except for the letters of Paul on the needs of the moment, the writings we now recognize as the New Testament were quite slow to appear. And when they did appear, a high proportion were anonymous or pseudonymous, not signed works of acknowledged authority. Their obvious characteristics were not those of great literature, but rather those of a personal mode of address, the direct qualities belonging to the spoken word, preserved in an oral tradition.

As there was already in existence a collection of written scriptures, even radical teachers like the Pharisees did not try to rewrite scripture. Instead they placed great emphasis on oral teaching and exposition, as a method of applying scripture to the problems of the day. Similarly neither John the Baptist nor Jesus himself appears to have recorded any teaching in the permanent form of writing. In this Jesus Christ was unlike Muhammad and other founders or reformers of religion. John the

Baptist and Jesus shared an extreme sense of urgency in their message and mission to 'this generation'. The appropriate medium for urgent communication was the short oracular utterance of prophecy; the more impersonal and protracted medium of formal writing seems almost to have been precluded by the situation.

The preaching of Jesus was controlled by the expectation of the Reign or Kingdom of God, and a belief that it was on the point of happening. In this Jesus did indeed stand in a line of continuity with Jewish expectations, without necessarily being committed to their more nationalistic expressions. He never spoke of a political Messiah who would destroy the enemies of Israel, nor of the establishment of a Jewish world-empire. But Jesus' expectations were cosmic in dimension, and world-wide in their effectiveness, without participating in the more fantastic speculations of the apocalyptic writers. Jesus' message was the proclamation that the fulfilment of past promises was at hand, that the Reign of God was initiated. The time of the long-expected climax was near:

> Blessed are the eyes that see what you see! For I tell you that many prophets and kings desired to see what you see, but did not see it, and to hear what you hear, but did not hear it. (Luke 10.23–4)

While the content of Jesus' message had been about God's kingdom, the focus of the first Christians' message was Jesus himself. This was the good news they felt compelled to share; this was the person to whom they were bound to bear witness. The message was not simply about a carpenter/teacher who had been executed under the Roman procurator. It was a joyful announcement of the long-awaited salvation of the Jews. For in the person of Jesus – identified as Christ, the Messiah – God had come to the rescue of a world in need. Because this *was* good news, it is not surprising that the content of the early Christian message gradually became known as 'the good news' (= the gospel = τό εὐαγγέλιον). Only later did this term come to be used of the documents in which the stories of Jesus were eventually recorded, that is the written gospels. The term 'good news' was primarily applied to the events concerning Jesus, and to the action of the early Christians in announcing those events (see Mark 1.1; 1 Corinthians 15.1).

When, much later, in the second century CE, the term 'gospel' or 'good news' was apparently first applied to a book or books, such as the 'memoirs of the apostles' (as Justin Martyr called them), it was felt necessary to lay stress on the identity of the written with the preached gospel, the essential continuity between these two modes of communication. It was the evidence of the historical record in these books which confirmed the truth of what the earliest Christians had preached, and this in turn corresponded with the prophecies of the Old Testament. Such second-century valuation placed upon the written works shows that the gospel preaching was now well on the way to becoming scripture. It was not only to be scripture in its own right, but also and particularly scripture attested by proofs from the authority of earlier scripture.

The sequence of events can be summarized in this way:

- Jesus proclaims the Reign/Kingdom of God (the prophecies of the Old Testament scripture are being fulfilled).
- The early Christians proclaim Jesus (the prophecies of the Old Testament scripture are applied directly to Jesus himself – this is a *new* interpretation).
- The Christian proclamation becomes scripture (the Old Testament scripture is clearly regarded as the *Old* Testament).

What eventually took place was precisely what could hardly have been conceived in the earliest days of the Church, namely the creation of a second Bible, to go alongside what was already in existence. Ultimately the second Bible would relegate the first (prophetic) scripture to the status of 'old' within a Bible composed of two testaments. The story of the development of the New Testament is the history of a process by which books, written for the most part for other purposes and with different motives, came to be accorded this unique status. And later hands imposed upon the New Testament a fixity and a sense of doctrinal unity which originally it could not be imagined to possess.

Christian Interpretation of the Old Testament

In the second century CE Justin Martyr makes a case for the superiority of his Christian philosophy in his *Dialogue with Trypho* (a Jew); he appeals to the Old Testament as evidence of God's plan that Judaism should be superseded by Christianity. Essentially the Jewish scriptures belong to the Christians because they point directly to Christ:

> The words which I use are not my own, nor are they embellished by human rhetoric, but they are the words as David sang them, as Isaiah announced them as good news, as Zachariah proclaimed them, and as

Moses wrote them. Aren't you acquainted with them, Trypho? You should be, for they are contained in your Scriptures, or rather not yours, but ours. For we believe and obey them, whereas you, though you read them, do not grasp their spirit.[3]

The following are examples of the relationship with the Old Testament that is set up in New Testament writings:

'Look, the virgin shall conceive and bear a son,
   and they shall name him Emmanuel,'
which means, 'God is with us.'   (Matthew 1.23 = Isaiah 7.14)

Out of Egypt I have called my son.   (Matthew 2.15 = Hosea 11.1)

Like a sheep he was led to the slaughter,
   and like a lamb silent before its shearer,
   so he does not open his mouth.
In his humiliation justice was denied him.
   Who can describe his generation?
      For his life is taken away from the earth.   (Acts 8.32–3 = Isaiah 53.7–8)

The one who is righteous will live by faith. (Romans 1.17 = Habakkuk 2.4)

What are human beings that you are mindful of them,
   or mortals [Gk. the son of man], that you care for them?
                             (Hebrews 2.6 = Psalm 8.4)

Significant differences may be apparent immediately between the Old and New Testament wordings of these texts. In addition, in the last example the political correctness of a modern translation (New Revised Standard Version) can be seen to obscure the connection. The indices contained in the present volume will allow the reader to cross-check the references in both directions. One can also see the relative frequency, or infrequency, of the use of particular Old Testament proof-texts. The example quoted from Acts, referring to the suffering servant figure in Isaiah, represents an almost automatic choice among Christians of later generations seeking a prophecy of Jesus in the Old Testament. But it should be pointed out that in the New Testament this Isaiah reference is surprisingly rarely used.[4]

Old Testament texts are cited in a variety of ways by the New Testament writers:

- Sometimes quotations are made directly (and accurately) from the original Hebrew or from a Greek translation; where variant readings exist between versions of the Old Testament text, the actual version used may then be identified accurately.
- Sometimes quotations are made from memory, or from an existing collection of proof-texts or testimonies, and so the wording may therefore only be approximate, and not tied to a particular version as source.
- Sometimes there is an allusion to an Old Testament theme or motif, rather than an exact quotation from the text, so that a symbol effectively carries the entire weight of a Biblical echo.
- Sometimes the quotation is not accurately attributed (as would be expected with a modern reference) – see, for example, Mark 1.2.
- Sometimes the Old Testament is misquoted (as in Matthew 27.9 for example), or its emphasis deliberately modified, in order to make the Christian meaning clearer.
- Sometimes a modern reader would feel that the quotation has been invalidated, simply because it has been taken out of context, or misapplied.

Equally there is a variety of reasons why New Testament writers have quoted, or alluded to, the Old Testament tradition. It may be

- to derive traditional rules for Christian living and substantiate them in moral exhortation;
- to support an argument for Jesus as the fulfilment of prophecy (e.g. as Messiah);
- to make the case for the church as the eschatological community of the new Israel;
- to use the Old Testament as a quarry for ultimate truths, the source of allegorical themes.

Depending to some extent on the reasons for quoting it, and on the nature of the Christian group for whom the quotation is made, there are also different ways in which a Christian interpretation of an Old Testament text or theme may be made. The presupposition underlying all of them is that there exists some kind of correspondence, or a typological relationship, between the Old and the New. Here are examples of four methods which are found frequently in the New Testament.

1 Promise and Fulfilment

The Old Testament text is used as an historical prototype, so that any part of the Old Testament can become a prophecy which the New Testament writers saw as fulfilled in their own day. The Qumran community used a similar method of interpretation (called *pesher*). The prophecy could be effectively rewritten in terms of the new situation; this was not thought to be taking liberties, but rather to be disclosing the ultimate meaning of the prophecy for the first time. An example is the use of Hosea 11.1 in Matthew 2.15. Hosea was describing the loving fatherhood of God, as demonstrated in Israel's historically formative experience at the Exodus from Egypt (see Exodus 4.22–3). Matthew uses the prophecy of Hosea in the story of Jesus' birth, to describe the flight into Egypt and the temporary refuge of the Holy Family there. Matthew has hijacked this prophecy from its original context for two reasons. It is a radical restatement, to show the importance of the rescue of the child Jesus from Herod; that is, it is a saving event on the same scale as Israel's Exodus. It is also an assertion about Jesus as 'Son of God'; this is the perfect fulfilment of the Father–Son relationship which was prefigured in the ideal commitment of Israel to God.

2 An Association of Old Testament Texts

A New Testament writer could construct an argument on the basis of the conjunction of several Old Testament texts, in the way that the Jewish rabbis did. This process worked by strict rules which permitted the making of analogies, drawing an inference from a lesser situation to a greater, or making a general application from an immediately preceding particular case. An example is the extended argument in 2 Corinthians 3, which is based on the narrative of Exodus 34 in combination principally with Jeremiah 31.31. Moses had to wear a veil, so as not to terrify the Israelites; but the veil also concealed the fact that the radiance waned. Moses' splendour waxed when he was in contact with God on the mountain top; when he came away it waned. The glory of the Mosaic covenant, based on letters carved in stone, was an alternating (waxing and waning) glory. Some Jews are similarly blindfolded and fail to recognize this. But, according to Paul's argument, the glory of the New Covenant grows steadily, and no veils are necessary. The apostle can constantly reflect the glory with ever-increasing brilliance, since (through Jesus Christ) God is constantly present as spirit.

INTRODUCTION

3 An Edifying Story

The Old Testament example can function as a salutary story, from which warning lessons can be drawn. A similar principle is seen to operate in the parables which Jesus told: the story is a striking way to focus attention on the moral which is to be drawn. So in 1 Corinthians 10.1–11 the stories of Israel's Exodus from Egypt, the crossing of the Red Sea, and the feeding in the wilderness, are applied to the Christian church: 'These things happened to them to serve as an example, and they were written down to instruct us, on whom the ends of the ages have come. So if you think you are standing, watch out that you do not fall' (10.11–12). Ultimately these stories serve as a warning for the Church of the last days, and emphasize the proper use of the sacraments of baptism and eucharist within the Church. The people of God can rely only on the security which their faith gives them. In the same way the story of Noah's ark is used in 1 Peter 3.20–1. Just as a few persons in the time of Noah were saved by means of the ark, so in the Church (the ark of God) the believing people of God experience the process of salvation, initiated by means of the rite of baptism.

4 Allegory and Spiritual Reading

Other readers of the Old Testament do not rest at the historical level (of precedents in the story of Israel) or at the level of moral teaching (edifying stories): they see a yet deeper spiritual meaning even in incidental features of the Old Testament. Elements are abstracted from the narrative, to become timeless, spiritual truths. Like dry tinder they catch fire with the spark of the allegorical method and blaze up as freely imaginative interpretations. The Church fathers of Alexandria were among the first to produce a structured system of levels of meaning in scripture (literal, moral and spiritual), by analogy with human psychology (body, soul and spirit). And they found proof-texts in the Bible to justify their method (e.g. the Septuagint Greek version of Proverbs 22.20: 'Describe these things in a threefold way'). As a result, any Old Testament reference to Jerusalem could mean (literally) the city of Judah; (morally) a faithful Christian soul; or, most significant of all, (spiritually) the Church of Christ – ultimately the heavenly city, New Jerusalem. But this is not just a matter of the later interpretations of the Church fathers. It is found even in the New Testament, for example in the interpretation of the parable of the sower (Mark 4.14–20), in the identification of the characters in Jesus' parable of the vineyard (Mark 12.1–11), and in Paul's letter to the Galatians (4.22–6). In Paul's allegorical reading (and reversal) of Old Testament history, Hagar stands for the old Israel and historical Jerusalem, while Sarah stands for the new Israel, the Church.

A process of interpretation, of one kind or another, is required, because the Old Testament references are not self-evident, although some are more familiar and obvious than others (for audiences within the Christian tradition). The Ethiopian who reads from the prophet Isaiah does not understand the application of the text. To Philip's question, 'Do you understand what you are reading?', he replies: 'How can I, unless someone guides me?' So Philip rides in his chariot with him, and beginning with the text of Isaiah 53, 'he proclaimed to him the good news about Jesus' (Acts 8.30–5). The techniques of Christian interpretation, which relate the teaching of the Old Testament and the preaching of the Christian gospel, are illustrated especially in Matthew. And the evangelist records the saying about the Christian interpreter:

> Therefore every scribe who has been trained for the kingdom of heaven is like the master of a household who brings out of his treasure *what is new and what is old*. (Matthew 13.52)

The Contents of this Volume

This volume is in two parts: a listing of the basic data on Old Testament quotation in the New Testament, and a small selection of critical essays which will illustrate the various academic methods of approach and some of the differing attitudes to be found in modern scholarship. In this way students are provided with the basic evidence and a sense of the scale of the debate in which they can join. The listing consists of two indices, both of them following the pattern of the appendices to Greek Testaments such as Nestle–Aland (27th edn). The first index concentrates principally on clear citations, grouped according to the books of the Old Testament. In the second index the same data are then reproduced in mirror image, as it were, classified according to the New Testament books. The two indices taken together provide a ready reference resource for tackling a range of problems in interpretation. In addition some of the most widely accepted and frequently identified allusions are also listed, while some of the more controversial possibilities are mentioned as examples within the interpretive essays, illustrating contrasting theories. More for the conventions of book production than for any sense of relative priority and importance, these indices are to be found at the rear of this volume.

INTRODUCTION

The four essays which follow each have their own declared purpose. Together it is hoped that they supply a perspective on the critical issues of this subject. The first essay, on the birth stories of Jesus, seeks to differentiate the formula quotations found in Matthew's gospel from the rather different genre of echoes of the Old Testament in the opening chapters of Luke's gospel. I have also invited contributions of a suitably multi-national kind from the American scholar Richard Hays and the English scholar Christopher Tuckett, who give widely contrasting estimates of the feasibility that a New Testament writer such as Paul should intend echoes of particular Old Testament texts in their contexts and expect the hearers to identify such echoes. A further essay, from the Dutch scholar Maarten Menken, provides a more extended introduction to the issues of methodology, using John's gospel as his working example. I have also included a book review from the *Journal of Theological Studies* in which I discuss briefly a theory that a New Testament text is being driven by specific citations of an Old Testament book and express my own preference for a more fluid approach, along such lines as a collective awareness in the Christian group of a 'living Bible'.

Maarten Menken's chapter is an excellent example of a working method for studying a New Testament writer's use of the Old Testament. What he writes about John's gospel represents a sequence of steps which might equally be applied to Matthew or Paul, for example. Menken works with direct quotations, indicated as such by an appropriate formula in the text. It is necessary to establish the dependence of these quotations upon Hebrew or Greek versions of the Old Testament. Menken illustrates by his working examples how one can see the New Testament writer modifying the Old Testament text, and he discusses the reasons why such modifications take place. It is possible to see how this method of studying Old Testament quotations can illuminate for us the theological concerns of the New Testament writer.

In the next contribution, Richard Hays asks, 'How did Paul read Isaiah?' His study concentrates on the frequency of Paul's quotations from, and allusions to, the canonical book of Isaiah the prophet, and he explores the reasons for Paul's special interest in this book. The suggestion is that the wider context of Isaiah's prophecies appealed to Paul, because he saw in it a foreshadowing of his own theology of the eschatological people of God. Paul's own vocation and mission could be said to be predicted by Isaiah, just as the Dead Sea Scrolls illustrate a similar use of Scripture to interpret the reasons for the existence of the

Qumran community. Christian readers of Paul's letters might be similarly trained to recognize and understand certain Scriptural motifs as applying to themselves. Hays offers a set of criteria by which this process can be assessed.

The third contribution, from Christopher Tuckett, is in debate with the position advocated by Richard Hays. Tuckett is unsure as to what extent any wider echoes of the Old Testament context would have been recognizable to Christian readers in the first century CE. His particular examples are drawn from instances in Paul's Corinthian correspondence. Given the different characteristics of the communities to which Paul wrote, one can recognize a statistical variation between the letters in Old Testament quotation and allusion. Paul as an effective communicator may well have allowed for a variation in his audience's abilities to pick up cross-references to traditional sources. The key historical question here is the spread of literacy, or more probably the recognition of how broad motifs and symbols, but not textual details, can be conveyed in a tradition of orality. A particularly interesting example used by Tuckett is that of first-century familiarity with the theme of Hannah's song (as in the Septuagint version of 1 Kingdoms 2). Paul may be able to criticize such a theme as manipulated by the Corinthians; subsequent readers of the New Testament would also recognize the echoes of Hannah in Mary's story and song within Luke 1.

Notes

1 Francis Watson, *Text, Church and World: Biblical Interpretation in Theological Perspective*, Edinburgh: T & T Clark, 1994, p. 3.
2 The rest of this section follows closely the line of argument in the introductory chapter of J. M. and K. M. Court, *The New Testament World*, Englewood Cliffs, NJ: Prentice-Hall and Cambridge: Cambridge University Press, 1990. It is recast with permission, for three reasons: the original work is no longer in print; it provides a basic summary of the historical situation; and it demonstrates how the argument of the present volume develops naturally from earlier work.
3 Justin, *Dialogue with Trypho* 29.2, as quoted in Bart D. Ehrman, *After the New Testament*, New York and Oxford: Oxford University Press, 1999, p. 111.
4 See Morna Hooker, *Jesus and the Servant: The Influence of the Servant Concept of Deutero-Isaiah in the New Testament*, London: SPCK, 1959.

2

The Birth of Jesus Christ According to Matthew and Luke

> In the Old Testament the New lies hid; in the New Testament the meaning of the Old becomes clear. (Augustine of Hippo)

One of the most striking ways to investigate the differences of emphasis and technique between New Testament writers in their use of the Old Testament is to compare the narratives of the birth of Jesus in the opening chapters of the gospels of Matthew and Luke. In this endeavour the unrivalled guide is an American Roman Catholic scholar, the late Raymond Brown, with his comparative commentary *The Birth of the Messiah*.[1]

The shared intention of Matthew and Luke in this regard is to unlock the Jewish traditions as the context in which the coming of Jesus could be interpreted and understood. In the words of Jonathan Z. Smith,

> Tension between the familiar and the unfamiliar, at the very heart of Judaism, has enormous cognitive power. It invites, it requires comparison. Judaism is foreign enough for comparison and interpretation to be necessary; it is close enough for comparison and interpretation to be possible.[2]

The differences between Matthew and Luke in their technique and style are due almost entirely to the differences between their cultural contexts (which they as evangelists share with their audience and readers). Matthew writes as a reforming teacher within a Jewish milieu, while Luke is interpreting the Jewish ethos of the Old Testament for a predominantly Gentile, Graeco-Roman readership.[3] The former task calls for a detailed examination of those texts which constitute the proof of the reforming teaching; the latter task requires a broader perspective and the ability to recreate in words a whole context of thought. Small wonder then if the effects of their respective uses of the Old Testament differ so greatly.

John Drury offered a similar contrast, but with some differences of emphasis, when he wrote:

> *Matthew* is Jewish, a close-neighbour of the Tannaitic rabbis who did their casuistic moralising out of scripture and the sayings of the wise. He lives as it were next door to them and quarrels with them stridently. *Luke* is Jewish in the story-telling tradition of the books of Genesis, Judges, Samuel and Kings, and the tales in the Apocrypha, a tradition still alive in Josephus.[4]

At about the same time the Swiss theologian Eduard Schweizer wrote, in his commentary on Matthew,

> Matthew and Luke both bear witness to this miracle [of Jesus' birth] in the manner appropriate to their belief in Jesus as Christ. Their accounts are therefore largely in agreement in what they are really trying to say, but are historically irreconcilable.[5]

The historical problem remains today, despite extensive research on astronomical data (seeking to identify the star which attracted the magi), or classical evidence for a census implemented by Quirinius, which might have any bearing on the date of Christ's birth. Such historical difficulties are only partially obscured by the modern preference for a more literary reading of the texts. In the story of Christ's birth, Matthew recounts nothing that is found in Luke's narrative, and vice versa. Even the angelic communication comes to Joseph in Matthew but to Mary in Luke. The only points of direct agreement between the two gospels are the fact that Jesus was born of a virgin in Bethlehem, and the statement that the names of his parents were Joseph and Mary. But in theological terms, which the use of the Old Testament greatly helps to articulate, there are much more important points of contact and direct comparison.

Genealogy as Old Testament Interpretation[6]

Two of Matthew's Old Testament proof-texts have already been mentioned in the introductory chapter, but before we look at this evidence, and at Luke's Old Testament style of poetry and narrative, we should pause at their genealogies (see Figure 1.1). The importance of this Old Testament historical perspective, at least for Matthew, is demonstrated by the fact that it occupies the opening verses of his gospel. From the outset Matthew uses the Old Testament to demonstrate the connection of past promise and present fulfilment in an historical perspective. He speaks of one in whom God's promises, delineated in the Old Testament, are now fulfilled. This is the one for whom the nations have longed (Matthew 4.12–16). The Christ is the one who gives a wholly new meaning to the Jewish concept of righteousness (Matthew 3.14–15). The presentation of Christ, as the goal of God's history and theological purpose, is conveyed in the genealogy, assembled largely on the basis of the Greek Bible (the Septuagint): from 1 Chronicles 2.1–15 and Ruth 4.18–22 for the pre-Davidic sequence, and from 1 Chronicles 3.5–16 for the post-Davidic. The sequence from Abraham, the father of the Jews, through King David, to Jesus the Messiah, is the demonstration of the logical outcome of God's history. Matthew's theme is emphasized at 1.1 and 1.17; as recipients of the promise Abraham and David provide thematic and not simply historical links.

Such a genealogy belongs within the traditions of learned Jewish exegesis, as practised by the teacher of the Torah who (according to Ecclesiasticus 39.3) 'seeks out the hidden meaning of parables and occupies himself with the obscurities of parables'. The point is in the outcome, with the Messiah as the climax of a schematic sequence. As Matthew 1.17 reveals, there are (or should be) three sequences of fourteen generations: from Abraham to David, from David to Jechoniah, and from Jechoniah to Jesus. With such a pattern of 42 generations ($42 = 6 \times 7$), it is left for the Messiah to commence the theologically significant seventh group of sevens. In confirmation of such esoteric patterns of thought, one should notice that the arithmetic total of the letters in the name of David, when numbers are assigned to the three Hebrew consonants in the name according to the principles of *gematria* (the letter/number symbolism found in Hebrew and other ancient languages), is itself the number 14, so important to Matthew's scheme.

While Matthew's hermeneutical concern is focused on Jesus as the Son of David, Luke's interest would seem to be significantly different. Luke's genealogy (3.23–38), differently located, after Jesus' baptism and at the start of his public ministry, indicates that Jesus is ultimately 'Son of God' (3.38). The coming of Jesus is not simply the fulfilment of the promises of Old Testament history; his ancestry is traced backwards (the flow is the reverse of Matthew's) not only as far as Abraham, but back

Matthew 1.1–17

¹ An account of the genealogy[a] of Jesus the Messiah,[b] the son of David, the son of Abraham.

² Abraham was the father of Isaac, and Isaac the father of Jacob, and Jacob the father of Judah and his brothers, ³ and Judah the father of Perez and Zerah by Tamar, and Perez the father of Hezron, and Hezron the father of Aram, ⁴ and Aram the father of Aminadab, and Aminadab the father of Nahshon, and Nahshon the father of Salmon, ⁵ and Salmon the father of Boaz by Rahab, and Boaz the father of Obed by Ruth, and Obed the father of Jesse, ⁶ and Jesse the father of King David.

And David was the father of Solomon by the wife of Uriah, ⁷ and Solomon the father of Rehoboam, and Rehoboam the father of Abijah, and Abijah the father of Asaph,[c] ⁸ and Asaph[d] the father of Jehoshaphat, and Jehoshaphat the father of Joram, and Joram the father of Uzziah, ⁹ and Uzziah the father of Jotham, and Jotham the father of Ahaz, and Ahaz the father of Hezekiah, ¹⁰ and Hezekiah the father of Manasseh, and Manasseh the father of Amos,[e] and Amos[f] the father of Josiah, ¹¹ and Josiah the father of Jechoniah and his brothers, at the time of the deportation to Babylon.

¹² And after the deportation to Babylon: Jechoniah was the father of Salathiel, and Salathiel the father of Zerubbabel, ¹³ and Zerubbabel the father of Abiud, and Abiud the father of Eliakim, and Eliakim the father of Azor, ¹⁴ and Azor the father of Zadok, and Zadok the father of Achim, and Achim the father of Eliud, ¹⁵ and Eliud the father of Eleazar, and Eleazar the father of Matthan, and Matthan the father of Jacob, ¹⁶ and Jacob the father of Joseph the husband of Mary, of whom Jesus was born, who is called the Messiah.[g]

¹⁷ So all the generations from Abraham to David are fourteen generations; and from David to the deportation to Babylon, fourteen generations, and from the deportation to Babylon to the Messiah,[h] fourteen generations.

Luke 3.23–38

²³ Jesus was about thirty years old when he began his work. He was the son (as was thought) of Joseph son of Heli, ²⁴ son of Matthat, son of Levi, son of Melchi, son of Jannai, son of Joseph, ²⁵ son of Mattathias, son of Amos, son of Nahum, son of Esli, son of Naggai, ²⁶ son of Maath, son of Mattathias, son of Semein, son of Josech, son of Joda, ²⁷ son of Joanan, son of Rhesa, son of Zerubbabel, son of Shealtiel,[i] son of Neri, ²⁸ son of Melchi, son of Addi, son of Cosam, son of Elmadam, son of Er, ²⁹ son of Joshua, son of Eliezer, son of Jorim, son of Matthat, son of Levi, ³⁰ son of Simeon, son of Judah, son of Joseph, son of Jonam, son of Eliakim, ³¹ son of Melea, son of Menna, son of Mattatha, son of Nathan, son of David, ³² son of Jesse, son of Obed, son of Boaz, son of Sala,[j] son of Nahshon, ³³ son of Amminadab, son of Admin, son of Arni,[k] son of Hezron, son of Perez, son of Judah, ³⁴ son of Jacob, son of Isaac, son of Abraham, son of Terah, son of Nahor, ³⁵ son of Serug, son of Reu, son of Peleg, son of Eber, son of Shelah, ³⁶ son of Cainan, son of Arphaxad, son of Shem, son of Noah, son of Lamech, ³⁷ son of Methuselah, son of Enoch, son of Jared, son of Mahalaleel, son of Cainan, ³⁸ son of Enos, son of Seth, son of Adam, son of God.

---

a Or *birth*
b Or *Jesus Christ*
c Other ancient authorities read *Asa*
d Other ancient authorities read *Asa*
e Other ancient authorities read *Amon*
f Other ancient authorities read *Amon*
g Or *the Christ*
h Or *the Christ*
i Gk *Salathiel*
j Other ancient authorities read *Salmon*
k Other ancient authorities read *Amminadab, son of Aram*; others vary widely

Figure 1.1   The genealogies of Christ in Matthew and Luke

to the first man, Adam. Such theological priorities are far more important in comparing the two genealogies than the seemingly fruitless attempts to harmonize the lists of names. Even if Luke's account is focused on Mary, while Matthew's has Joseph as a central character, there is no simple explanation such as that Luke gives the wife's genealogy and Matthew the husband's. At this level the historical considerations are in tension with the theological: both gospels stress the importance of the virginal conception, while both genealogies seem to operate through Joseph.

To quote Raymond Brown's conclusions:

> The Lucan list, while in some ways more plausible than Matthew's list, scarcely constitutes an exact record of Jesus' biological ancestry. . . . What one may say with surety of Luke's list is that, in part, it is artificially arranged in numerical patterns of seven and that it contains enough inaccuracies and confusions to suggest a popular provenance . . . among Greek-speaking Jews. Luke adopted this list and adapted it for theological purposes by placing it between the baptism of Jesus and his temptations. . . . If his is the only genealogy in the Bible to trace a man's origins to God, that is because his genealogy comes after the baptism where a voice from heaven proclaimed Jesus as God's Son.[7]

Matthew's Use of Formula Quotations

The Introduction to this volume has already mentioned what may well be Matthew's own self-description as a 'scribe trained for the kingdom of heaven' (13.52, special to Matthew). The modern scholar O. Lamar Cope, who first applied this text to Matthew himself, explained its meaning in this way:

> The author of the gospel of Matthew . . . was a Jewish-Christian author thoroughly familiar with the Old Testament and with Jewish traditions of its interpretation. He employed this knowledge as a key to the organization of a number of the parts of his gospel. . . . He especially showed his understanding of the relationship between his Christian faith and the Old Testament, and the relationship of both to the problems of Christians of his own day. He was therefore 'a scribe'. . . . I do not mean that it can be shown that Matthew was actually a Jewish scribe, or that he had been trained as one, although both might be true. I do think that Matthew would not have objected to this description of himself.[8]

Among the Old Testament quotations used by Matthew there is a distinctive group, marked out by the way that they are introduced with a precise formula ('in fulfilment of that which was spoken'). These are reflective quotations, interpreting the event, and summing up its significance at the end of the story, by the use of the Greek verb πληρόω. This category of formula quotation is widespread in the gospel from beginning to end, as Table 2.1 shows, but there are four clear instances at the outset, in the birth stories.

Table 2.1 Formula quotations in Matthew

1.22–23	Isaiah 7.14	Simple fulfilment text
2.15	Hosea 11.1	Clue to link with Moses
2.17–18	Jeremiah 31.15	Simple fulfilment text
2.23	?Isaiah 11.1/?Judges 13.5	Disputed source, but key text for Nazareth move
4.14–16	Isaiah 9.1–2	Validates start of ministry
8.17	Isaiah 53.4	Applies inclusively to healings
12.17–21	Isaiah 42.1–4	Jesus as the servant: structural importance for ch.12
13.14–15	Isaiah 6.9–10	Structural for theory and interpretation of parables
13.35	Psalm 78.2	Jesus as revealer of secrets through parables etc.
21.4–5	Zechariah 9.9 + Isaiah 62.11	Text as source of *two* animals in story
27.9–10	Zechariah 11.13 cited; ?influence of Jeremiah 19.1–13; cf. Jeremiah 32.6–9; 18.1–2	Interwoven texts to interpret Judas' fate

This group of proof-texts stands out by virtue of its specific and formulaic reference to fulfilment; the quotations may also be linked by observing the unusually mixed nature of the Old Testament texts used. But beyond this group there are many other Old Testament quotations in Matthew's gospel, which undoubtedly maintain this ethos of fulfilment, despite a less rigid introductory formula (see, for example, Matthew 2.5–6, 3.3, 11.10, 15.7–9, 21.42).

Other Old Testament Motifs in Matthew's Gospel

Matthew's use of the Old Testament is by no means restricted to the explicit quotations and the reflective formulae of the proof-texts. Many aspects of the birth narratives invite comparison with Old Testament stories, in such a way as to suggest that the hearers or readers were expected to notice the parallels and allow the echoes to reverberate within their own understanding of the story. Matthew's intention appears to be to build theologically upon such typological links. The cue provided to stimulate such recognition may be a name, a detail, or the comparability of circumstances.

The actual name of Joseph offers the first indication: Mary's betrothed seems a far cry from the Old Testament patriarch of that name, but as Joseph in Canaan and Egypt had a reputation as a dreamer (and interpreter of dreams), so in Matthew's narrative there are five explicit references to dreams, four of which are specifically directed at the New Testament Joseph (Matthew 1.20, [2.12], 2.13, 2.19, 2.22). The motif of the star which attracts the astrologers (or wise men) – Matthew 2.2 – invites comparison with Balaam's vision of the star out of Jacob (Numbers 24.15–17) – a passage which undoubtedly conveyed messianic/christological ideas for some early Christians, as depicted in the Roman catacombs. A third echo, which may take on even greater significance later in the gospel (with Matthew's picture of Jesus as the law-giver), is that of the life of Moses, where there are correspondences in the details of the early life: the birth and naming, the persecution, escape and return. If Moses stands as prototype for Jesus, so Pharaoh corresponds to King Herod.

In such ways the theological statements about Jesus are built up from Old Testament precedent. And so the story Matthew tells is not simply a narrative of the birth and early years, but also a declaration of the birth of the Messiah, transforming Old Testament prototypes and precedents. Such intentions are confirmed by the co-existence of explicit proof-texts emphasizing fulfilment, but Matthew's additional and wider creativity in narrative, with its foundation in the Old Testament, suggests other methods of interpretation which Luke also can use.

Explicit Christology in Matthew and in Luke

For both Matthew and Luke, Jesus is 'Saviour', but the way this is expressed is significantly different. Compare Matthew 1.21 ('She will bear a son, and you are to name him Jesus, for he will save his people from their sins', followed by the reflective proof-text from Isaiah 7.14, quoted in Matthew 1.23) with Luke 1.31 ('And now, you will conceive in your womb and bear a son, and you will name him Jesus'). Matthew explains the name Jesus (or Joshua) by its popular etymology (as meaning 'Yahweh is salvation') in the last part of verse 21. Such an explanation would only be comprehensible to a reader with knowledge of Hebrew, but Matthew seems to presuppose this. By the New Testament period the echo of meaning in the name Jesus, rather than being explicitly theophoric, would probably be restricted to the basic idea of saviour, but this meaning would be widely recognized.

Luke in turn seems to presuppose the text of Isaiah 7.14 as an allusion underlying what he writes in 1.31, but he does not actually quote the text. Does he also presuppose that his readers will know the etymology of the name Jesus? This is unlikely, as the name is simply stated as a fact and seems rather to be taken for granted. To appreciate Luke's theology, it is more important to notice the frequent use he makes in the birth stories of the nouns 'saviour' and 'salvation' (as applied to Jesus e.g. in Luke 1.69, 2.11, 2.30). In contrast Matthew does not use the noun 'saviour' applied directly to Jesus.

Among the texts just listed, Luke 2.11 warrants special notice, indicating the terms in which Jesus is announced by the angel to the shepherds: 'to you is born this day in the city of David a Saviour, who is the Messiah, the Lord.' These final elements can well be translated alternatively as 'Messiah and Lord' or 'Christ the Lord' or 'Anointed Lord', or regarded as possibly a mistranslation or copyist's error for 'Lord's Anointed' or 'Messiah of the Lord God', as found at Luke 2.26. It is tempting to think that Luke is using the earliest Christian titles, but that he has assembled them into a solemn formula appropriate for an imperial proclamation (which suits the way that he has contextualized the birth of Christ within the world of the Roman empire; see Luke 2.1). In this way, just as in the titles of Jesus in the book of Revelation, the rival claims of the Son of God and of the Emperor as earthly lord and master are settled in the confident view of Luke the evangelist in favour of Jesus as God's Son. The formula used also invites comparison with that of Philippians 3.20, applied to Christ's Second Coming. But one should not forget the comparable Jewish pattern of messianic titles, as in Isaiah 9.6.

Luke's Septuagintal Style

Like Matthew, Luke equally operates with Old Testament themes, but he can use them in several rather different ways. The themes colour the language he uses to tell the story; they are set out in the songs which he includes within the story; they are present in the characters of his story, such as prophets and shepherds, and are focused by powerful symbols used repeatedly.

Luke appears as an accomplished writer in the Hellenistic world of letters within the Roman empire; as such, he invites comparison with the Jewish historian and apologist Josephus when he wrote for a Roman readership. The opening chapters of Luke's gospel, the birth stories, may seem to stand apart from the rest of the gospel, because of their explicit or more self-conscious atmosphere of the Old Testament. Such a contrast may be more apparent than real. In the world of Graeco-Roman letters there was undoubtedly a special appeal of the exotic, comparable with the much more modern attractions of Orientalism. In such a context of Hellenistic syncretism, there had been a renaissance of an Old Testament style of historiography, as is also seen in the pages of Josephus. So for reasons of historical authenticity, and also of marketing interest, the birth of Jesus (and the parallel birth of John the Baptist) is set in an Old Testament context, formulated by the expressions of one particular Greek translation of the Hebrew Bible, the Septuagint from Alexandria. In Howard Marshall's words, 'The birth narrative reflects a piety nourished upon the Old Testament, and the action of God recounted in it is depicted in Septuagintal terminology.'[9] Or according to Adolf von Harnack, 'The whole style is artificial and is intended to produce an impression of antiquity – a purpose which has been really fulfilled.'[10]

Perhaps the most striking example of correspondence between Luke's account and the Septuagint is the relationship between Mary's song (the Magnificat) in Luke 1.46–55 and the song of Hannah in 1 Samuel (1 Kingdoms) 2.1–10. It could be said that the words Luke gives to Mary are 'modelled in general terms on 1 Samuel . . . but the phrases used are paralleled in many passages, and the hymn gives the impression of being composed by someone whose mind was steeped in Old Testament piety.'[11] Earlier discussion of the relation between Luke's writing and the Thanksgiving Hymns (*Hodayoth*) among the Dead Sea Scrolls concluded that the only link was in the general Old Testament heritage which they had in common. But there is more to the relationship between the songs of Mary and Hannah, as any student who grapples with the (more difficult) Greek of the Septuagint will discover: compare especially 1 Samuel 1.11 and Luke 1.48; 1 Samuel 2.1–2 and Luke 1.46–7; 1 Samuel 2.7–8 and Luke 1.51–3. In addition the literary history is similar, with two hymns, as more general compositions, inserted into their respective narratives. And the thematic parallelism between Mary and Hannah can be carried forward into Luke 2, when Mary brings Jesus to the Temple as Hannah brought Samuel to the Tabernacle at Shiloh (1 Samuel 1.24).

The Impact of Luke's Interpretation of the Old Testament

Each of the hymns, or canticles, in Luke's opening chapters has raised questions about its literary origins and inspiration. Along with Mary's song, those of Zechariah (the Benedictus, Luke 1.68–79) and of Simeon (the Nunc Dimittis, Luke 2.29–32) are seen as originating within a reflective Old Testament tradition, even possibly being formulated as hymns in the Maccabean period. The traditional ethos is clearly indicated, even if exact proof of origin is never likely to be established. Here one can see the real significance of the comparison between Luke's interpretation of the Old Testament and Matthew's proof-texts that emphasize fulfilment. The medium is technically different, but the theological intention is very similar. Matthew uses direct quotations which interpret the event, summing up its significance as its climax; Luke employs in a more general way the sweep of Old Testament prophetic terminology, articulated in these songs. For Matthew past prophecies are seen as reaching fulfilment in the present; for Luke the new age has dawned and in this new beginning the future tenses of prophecy have been converted into the simple past tenses (the Greek aorist) of fulfilment. Similar manipulations of ancient texts, renewing them with new tenses and pronouns, can be observed in the Dead Sea Scrolls (particularly 11Q Torah or the Temple Scroll). The theme of new age and new creation is seen at the heart of the narrative of Jesus' birth, in the activity of the Holy Spirit (Matthew 1.20; Luke 1.35: cf. Genesis 1.2; Joel 2.28). For Matthew the decisive terminology to define the person of Christ is the title 'Son of David'; for Luke the equivalent expression is 'Son of God'.

The Old Testament tradition, exemplified in the prophetic writings, and interpreted prophetically as a whole, is vital to an understanding of the evangelist's theology, in the gospel of Luke just as in that of Matthew. The characteristic of prophecy is heralding and explaining what is happening or about to happen. In the two opening chapters of Luke's gospel the characters otherwise known to Christians are written up from within the Gospel tradition, and those characters who are otherwise unknown are written up as Old Testament prophetic figures. So in the persons of Zechariah, Simeon and Anna the links with the Old Testament are reinforced and the message of promise and fulfilment is underlined.

The same could be said of the shepherds who respond to the angels' message. It is tempting to regard Luke's shepherds as the social gospel's point of contact with the working man, while Matthew's magi represent the professional classes, but the Old Testament background may be ultimately more significant than a modern sociological interpretation at this point. There is a long-standing symbolism in the Old Testament of the shepherd as leader (for good or bad) of the chosen people. Think of King David on the one hand, and on the other the false leaders targeted in Jeremiah 23, Ezekiel 34, Isaiah 40.10f., and Zechariah 11. This is a theme which reaches its climax in the 'parable' of the Good Shepherd in John 10.

A further example to demonstrate this continuity between the Old and New Testaments is the advance announcement of the birth of Jesus (and in parallel that of John the Baptist) in Luke's gospel. There appears to be a Biblical pattern,[12] appropriate to the announcement of a significant birth, to be seen (for example) with reference to Ishmael in Genesis 16, Isaac in Genesis 17, Samson in Judges 13, Samuel in 1 Samuel 1, and David's descendant in 2 Samuel 7. This may be announced by angels and interpreted by prophets or seers (as with the dynasty of David, prophesied by Nathan in 2 Samuel 7). Luke develops this pattern in the annunciation of Jesus' birth (1.26ff.): there is a description of the child and the future, the special circumstances of a virginal conception, and the obedient response of Mary in the supreme role-model of the faithful disciple. Luke's main purpose is to make explicit the theological interpretation, embracing, within the annunciation, statements about Christ from Christian preaching. One can compare the formulae Paul uses in Romans 1.3–4: 'the gospel concerning his Son, who was descended from David according to the flesh and was declared to be Son of God with power according to the spirit of holiness by resurrection from the dead, Jesus Christ our Lord.'

As a similar pattern is used in announcing to Joseph the birth of Jesus in Matthew 1.20ff., it would be possible to suggest the reconstruction of an early Christian tradition, evolved from the Old Testament, of such an annunciation by angelic messenger of the birth of Christ. Both evangelists would then have adapted such a pattern in the framework of their own theology. What is then particularly interesting in such a context is the development of ideas in Luke's gospel which yields the traditions in parallel of annunciation and birth for John the Baptist in Luke 1.11ff., and then for Jesus in Luke 1.26ff. This duplication is a quite unexpected aspect of Luke's presentation and cannot simply be explained with reference to Old Testament parallelism and repetition in narrative, because the parallel we are offered is between Jesus and John the Baptist, the prophecies of two lives, two careers, in relationship to one another. The annunciation of the birth of John the Baptist and the ensuing, intertwined narrative has been shaped deliberately by Luke.

By virtue of the active involvement of the Holy Spirit in both cases (1.15; 1.35), the type of true prophecy is ultimately revealed. Luke is making a statement about the ultimate truth of prophecy, and he uses Elijah as the type of the true prophet. Traditionally Elijah was expected to return, as one of the Old Testament figures who had been removed from this earth to God's immediate presence by supernatural means. He has a special cup waiting for him at the Jewish Passover. Conventional Christian interpretation saw Elijah returned in the person of John the Baptist, as the herald of Jesus himself. Luke's picture is not so straightforward; for him what Elijah represents as a forerunner is equally applicable to Jesus as the herald of God, and to John as the herald of Jesus. These roles are not mutually exclusive within the concept of prophecy and ultimate truth. And so the roles are set in parallel, running alongside each other in Luke's theological interpretation.

As John the Baptist – and in Luke's gospel, also Jesus himself – dramatize the classic role of Elijah the prophet (as forerunner of Jesus himself and of God, respectively), so the definitive signal is given by Luke, to enable his readers to recognize the fulfilment of all that the Old Testament has represented in anticipation. It is therefore entirely appropriate that, in Luke's picture of the birth of Jesus, the supporting characters (such as Simeon and Anna in Luke 2.25–8), as has been noted, are depicted in the guise of Old Testament prophets who comment on the action.

Notes

1 Raymond E. Brown, *The Birth of the Messiah: A Commentary on the Infancy Narratives in the Gospels of Matthew and Luke* (AB Reference Library), revd edn, New York: Doubleday, 1993.
2 Jonathan Z. Smith, *Imagining Religion*, Chicago, IL: Chicago University Press, 1988, p. xii.
3 For the documentation in support of this generalization, see J. M. and K. M. Court, *The New Testament World*, Englewood Cliffs, NJ: Prentice-Hall and Cambridge: Cambridge University Press, 1990, Chapters 3 and 4.
4 John Drury, *Tradition and Design in Luke's Gospel*, London: Darton, Longman & Todd, 1976, p. 8.
5 Eduard Schweizer, *The Good News according to Matthew*, London: SPCK, 1976, p. 32.
6 On this topic, see e.g. Marshall D. Johnson, *The Purpose of the Biblical Genealogies*, Cambridge: Cambridge University Press, 1969; Robert R. Wilson, *Genealogy and History in the Biblical World*, New Haven: Yale University Press, 1977.
7 Brown, *The Birth of the Messiah*, pp. 93–4, 90.
8 O. Lamar Cope, *Matthew: A Scribe Trained for the Kingdom of Heaven* (CBQMS 5), Washington: Catholic Bible Association, 1976, p. 10 and n. 36.
9 I. Howard Marshall, *Luke: Historian and Theologian*, Exeter: Paternoster Press, 1970, pp. 96–7.
10 Adolf von Harnack, *Luke the Physician*, London: Williams and Norgate, 1907, p. 217.
11 Howard Marshall, *Luke*, 1970, p. 97.
12 See Brown, *The Birth of the Messiah*, p. 156.

3

The Old Testament in the Book of Revelation: A Review of Two Books by G. K. Beale

The Book of Revelation. A Commentary on the Greek Text, pp. lxiv, 1245 (The New International Greek Testament Commentary), Grand Rapids, MI: Eerdmans/Carlisle: Paternoster Press, 1999

John's Use of the Old Testament in Revelation, pp. 443 (*Journal for the Study of the New Testament*, Supplement Series, 166), Sheffield Academic Press, 1999

These two books invite a joint review: they intersect and overlap substantially, each providing reinforcement for the arguments of the other. The commentary supplies illustration throughout the book of Revelation for Beale's thesis of Old Testament use, while the monograph substantiates in particular directions the theoretical aspects covered more briefly in the introduction to the commentary.

The modern trend, perhaps in sincere imitation of R. H. Charles, is for longer commentaries, the massive outcome of decades of study. G. K. Beale's work began from a Cambridge dissertation on Daniel, published in 1980. His commentary in excess of 1,300 pages is only succinct when compared with David Aune's three volumes, recently published in the Word Commentary series and set to establish themselves as the definitive commentary for today. The justification for treatment on such a scale rests in the polymorphic character of Revelation's text, the recognition that it requires a range of critical methodologies for an adequate understanding, and the need (which Beale specifically acknowledges) to attempt an assessment of the vast outpouring of

---

This essay was first published in *Journal of Theological Studies*, 51 (2000), pp. 295–7; reprinted with permission.

secondary literature on, or related to, Revelation, the fruits of late twentieth-century fascination with this text.

Beale's agenda is dominated by his special interest in the use of the Old Testament, not only in Revelation itself, but also comparatively, referring to similar allusions employed in the Jewish exegetical tradition. He also seeks precision in tracing the flow of Revelation's argument and summarizing it effectively for the use of today's worshipping community. So he rightly acknowledges the 'Church' focus in and for this text, while the historical questions about the early Johannine communities are given a lower priority than the older kinds of literary-critical questions, centred on the relationship to the Old Testament tradition.

He is fond of the word 'trenchant': 'study the Old Testament allusions in a more trenchant manner' and 'trace in a more trenchant manner the flow of thought'. Certainly trenchancy conveys a mood not a method, and suggests a combative and summarily dismissive approach to alternative interpretations. This would be fairly accurate in describing the treatment of some references to my work in the commentary!

Most studies of Old Testament allusions in Revelation are particularist: it is either Daniel that is used, or Ezekiel, or perhaps Isaiah, or Zechariah. But how is it possible to decide among several possibilities, when there is evidence for all? On the other hand, if the commentator is more inclusive in this regard, this raises interesting but possibly unanswerable questions about the way an early Christian community, with an ambivalent relation to Judaism, would have handled the scriptural traditions. But the problem with allusions, and with some theories about midrashic kinds of interpretation, is precisely that we are dealing with allusions, and *not* quotations, and therefore it is very hard to prove a precise relationship between Old and New Testament texts. Should it be a consistent exegesis, driven by an external text, or is the very allusiveness indicative of a looser, reflective, associative and meditative approach, adopted by one or many within the Christian community?

'The author could think of no better way to describe his visions than with language used by the OT prophets to describe similar visions.' Beale's hermeneutic is clearly author-centred: 'for John the Christ-event is the key to understanding the OT, and yet reflection on the OT context leads the way to further comprehension of this event and provides the redemptive-historical background against which the apocalyptic visions are better understood; the New Testament interprets the Old and the Old interprets the New.' The Seer's insights and the programme of spiritual education for his community are of course vital, but Beale is at his most trenchant in distrusting more modern techniques of literary criticism, such as reader-response or intertextuality, as ways of elucidating these texts.

My own preference would be for a more fluid and less authorial description of the process. The structure of visions in Daniel, and its recapitulation and structural influence in 4 Ezra as well as Revelation and elsewhere, may owe much to the creative insights and experience of individual writers, but it only succeeds as a process of literary communication because this is a tradition within which this religious community lives, and where ideas from the scriptural past may reverberate with their contemporary experience, evoking renewed patterns of understanding. For this reason I attach importance to the task of clarifying, as best we can, the scriptural milieu – let's call it 'the living Bible' – from all the comparative sources at our disposal. In this respect I felt that Beale understates and underuses the material from the Dead Sea Scrolls, and strangely does not seem to reflect the most recent Qumran scholarship.

4

Old Testament Quotations in the Gospel of John

Maarten J. J. Menken

The Old Testament in Early Christianity

The first followers of Jesus were Jews; the collection of writings that we call the Old Testament was their holy scripture. In those writings, they found a testimony of God's way with Israel in the past, a guide for what God wanted them to do in the present, and a source of hope for their future deliverance by God. As soon as they became convinced that with Jesus the Kingdom of God had come and that he was God's final messenger, they tried to legitimate this conviction with the help of the scriptures. If Jesus was the one by whom God realized his plan with Israel and with the world, this should in their view be demonstrable from scripture. Of course, they read the scriptures as first-century Jews read them: as the Word of God which was directly relevant to their own time and situation.

When increasingly non-Jews were joining the Christian communities, the scriptures remained the basis of Christian proclamation and theology: the first Christians assumed that these non-Jews shared in the realization of God's promises to Israel. When Paul reminds the Christian community of Corinth, which consisted for the greater part of former Gentiles (1 Corinthians 12.2), of his first proclamation, he says: 'For I delivered to you first of all that which I also received, that Christ died for our sins, in accordance with the Scriptures, and that he was buried, and that he was raised on the third day, in accordance with the Scriptures' (1 Corinthians 15.3–4). These phrases, apparently in use even before Paul, show that 'accordance with the Scriptures' was from the very beginning an essential part of Christian preaching and doctrine.

This article is a revised and expanded English version of 'Citaten uit het Oude Testament in het evangelie van Johannes (1,23; 2,17; 12,40; 19,36)', in G. Van Belle (ed.), *Het Johannesevangelie: Woorden om van te leven*, Leuven: Vlaamse Bijbelstichting and Leuven/ Amersfoort: Acco, 1995, pp. 71–86.

The Old Testament in the Fourth Gospel

In this light, it is not surprising that in the New Testament writings we meet numerous quotations from and allusions to the Old Testament. The gospel of John is no exception. One need not be a great biblical scholar to recognize in the opening words of this gospel an allusion to the beginning of the book of Genesis. 'In the beginning was the Word' (John 1.1) reminds one unmistakably of 'In the beginning God created the heaven and the earth' (Genesis 1.1). Many more examples can be found in the Fourth Gospel.[1]

In this paper, I will concentrate on what I would call the 'marked quotations' in John, that is, the more or less verbatim and thus easily recognizable renderings of a clause or a series of clauses from scripture, which are introduced or concluded by a formula that makes clear that the words in question come from scripture (e.g., 'as the prophet Isaiah said', John 1.23; 'that the Scripture might be fulfilled', John 13.18).[2] The following passages meet these criteria: 1.23 = Isaiah 40.3; 2.17 = Psalm 69.10; 6.31 = Psalm 78.24; 6.45 = Isaiah 54.13; 7.38 = Psalm 78.16, 20; 7.42 = 2 Samuel 7.12; Micah 5.1, etc.; 8.17 = Deuteronomy 19.15; 10.34 = Psalm 82.6; 12.15 = Zechariah 9.9; 12.34 = Psalm 89.37; 12.38 = Isaiah 53.1; 12.40 = Isaiah 6.10; 13.18 = Psalm 41.10; 15.25 = Psalm 69.5 (or Psalm 35.19); 19.24 = Psalm 22.19; 19.36 = Psalm 34.21 and Exodus 12.46; 19.37 = Zechariah 12.10. Apparently, the fourth evangelist has a special interest in the prophets Isaiah and Zechariah and in the Psalms, an interest that is by no means exceptional within the New Testament.

The generally short quotations (on average nine words) have various functions, and are used by various actors. John the Baptist indicates his position in the history of salvation by a quotation (1.23). Jesus makes use of quotations to show that his ministry is in agreement with the scriptures (6.45; 7.38; 13.18; 15.25). An action of Jesus reminds the disciples of a word from scripture (2.17). Jesus and his opponents use quotations in their disputes on the question who Jesus really is, to support their diverging points of view (6.31; 7.42; 8.17; 10.34; 12.34). The evangelist adduces quotations to establish that what he tells his audience about Jesus, especially about the end of Jesus' ministry, agrees with the scriptures and constitutes their fulfilment (12.15, 38, 40; 19.24, 36, 37).

The Provenance of the Old Testament Quotations in John

John's selection of Old Testament quotations was to a large extent determined by tradition. We find some of his quotations in parallel pericopae in the synoptic gospels. The words on 'the voice of one crying in the wilderness' from Isaiah 40.3 are applied to John the Baptist not only in John 1.23, but also in Matthew 3.3, Mark 1.3 and Luke 3.4. The prophecy about the king coming on a donkey from Zechariah 9.9 is connected to Jesus' entry into Jerusalem in both Matthew 21.5 and John 12.15, and it seems that it already influenced the entry narrative of Mark 11.1–10, which was the source of Matthew 21.1–9.

There are also a few instances in which John explicitly advances an Old Testament passage that is only alluded to in the synoptic parallels. According to Mark 14.18, Jesus announces at the Last Supper that 'the one who is eating with me' will betray him. This is an allusion to Psalm 41.10, and John explicitly quotes this psalm verse in his story of the washing of the disciples' feet (13.18). In the synoptic passion narratives, it is said, in an evident allusion to Psalm 22.19, that soldiers divide Jesus' clothes among themselves by casting lots (Matthew 27.35; Mark 15.24; Luke 23.34). John explicitly cites this psalm verse in his version of the incident (19.24). Whether one considers the gospel of John as directly dependent on the synoptic gospels or as dependent on the synoptic tradition, it is in any case obvious that the connection between precisely these Old Testament passages and these episodes from the story about Jesus had already been made before John.

In other cases, the evangelist appears to quote from Old Testament passages which are used elsewhere in the New Testament in a different context. I note the law of the two or three witnesses (Deuteronomy 19.15 = John 8.17; cf. Matthew 18.16; 2 Corinthians 13.1; 1 Timothy 5.19), the promise of a Davidic Messiah (2 Samuel 7.12 = John 7.42, cf. Acts 13.23 etc.), the 'hardening decree' (Isaiah 6.10 = John 12.40; cf. Matthew 13.13–15; Mark 4.12; Luke 8.10; Acts 28.27), the beginning of the song of the suffering servant of the Lord (Isaiah 53.1 = John 12.38; cf. Romans 10.16), the prophecy of the Messiah's provenance from Bethlehem (Micah 5.1 = John 7.42; cf. Matthew 2.6), the word on the pierced one on whom they will look (Zechariah 12.10 = John 19.37; cf. Revelation 1.7; Matthew 24.30), a fragment of one of the psalms of the righteous sufferer (Psalm 69.10 = John 2.17; cf. Romans 15.3, where Paul quotes the second half of the verse). So in his selection of Old Testament passages the fourth evangelist largely concurs with early

Christian tradition. Jesus' Messiahship was legitimated by certain Old Testament passages.[3] This observation, however, does not alter the fact that, as we shall see, John expresses his own, particular emphases in his editing of Old Testament quotations.

Old Testament Versions and John's Editorial Work

But how can we detect John's editorial work? To do so, we have to know what Old Testament text the evangelist used. If we do not know which version he used, we run the risk of ascribing either too much or not enough importance to his editorial work. Some historical and methodological considerations must be dealt with here.

In the time in which John's gospel originated, those who needed a Greek text of the Old Testament (Greek-speaking Jews and others) generally used the Septuagint (LXX), the Old Greek translation of the Old Testament. This translation was made in several stages during a period that extended from the third to the first century BCE. It differs in several respects from the Hebrew text as we know it, that is, the so-called Masoretic Text. As far as its consonants are concerned, the Masoretic Text is in essence the Hebrew text that was predominantly used at the end of the first century of our era. The differences between the LXX and the Masoretic Text are probably partly due to the use, by the Greek translators, of a different Hebrew text; but in part they are also the result of exegetical decisions by the translators. There is evidence that there also circulated, in the first century CE, revisions of the LXX. These revisions arose because of the differences between the LXX and the Hebrew text that was current at the time, and they represent a movement in the direction of this Hebrew text.

If there are clear differences between the Hebrew text and the LXX, it is relatively easy to determine whether or not John follows the LXX when quoting.[4] However, proximity to the Hebrew text does not automatically mean direct use of that text. John may have used a revision of the LXX. We can assume that John himself translated the Hebrew text if three conditions are met: (1) it must be impossible to trace the translation given in John's gospel back to the LXX or to a revision of it, (2) the translation must display the marks of John's hand, and (3) there must be a reason why he does not use the LXX. Of course, the LXX often gives a correct and obvious translation of the Hebrew. If John's text agrees in such a case with the LXX, there is, at least in theory, the possibility that he himself made the same correct and obvious translation of the Hebrew as the LXX translator did before him. One should then be attentive to elements of the Hebrew text that could be correctly translated into Greek in more than one way. When there is agreement in those elements between John's biblical text and the LXX, John apparently follows the LXX. This argument gains additional force when the translation in John deviates from the evangelist's usual vocabulary or style.

If we have detected which version of the Old Testament was used in a particular quotation, we can establish what modifications were made in the biblical text. Presupposing that a modification is deliberate, and that it was made by the evangelist (and not already at a prior stage of tradition), we should be able to explain it on the basis of John's literary and theological tendencies. In this context, we should take into account the fact that textual modification of a quotation can be the result of the use of certain hermeneutical devices current at the time. We know, for instance, that in pre-Christian Judaism, it was already considered legitimate to connect analogous passages from scripture (analogous passages are passages that have at least one word in common and that mostly also have similar content). This device was used not only in exegesis, but also in the rendering of texts: a part of the one could be used as a substitute for a part of the other, or could be added to it. We encounter this practice in various writings, among them the LXX itself, and the Qumran scrolls.[5] The LXX has, for instance, rendered the designation of God as a 'warrior' in Exodus 15.3 by 'one who breaks wars' (I translate literally). This happened under the influence of the Hebrew text of Psalm 76.4 and Hosea 2.20, where it is said that God 'has broken' or 'will break the war'; the connecting word which legitimizes the interpretation and translation of one text in accordance with the other is 'war'. A Johannine example (in John 19.36) will be discussed below. The use of such a hermeneutical device affords *legitimacy* to a textual change; the necessary next step is to look for the *motive* for the alteration.

Approaching the Old Testament quotations in John on the basis of the above methodological considerations gives the following results as far as the versions used are concerned. In eleven instances (1.23; 2.17; 6.31, 45; 7.38; 10.34; 12.15, 38; 15.25; 19.24, 36), we can be fairly sure that the evangelist drew his quotations from the LXX. John took two quotations partly or completely from the Hebrew text, which he probably translated himself (12.40 = Isaiah 6.10; 13.18 = Psalm 41.10). The quotation from Zechariah 12.10 in John 19.37 is a case apart: here, John makes use of the Greek translation which was current in early Christianity as a testimony about Jesus' final coming (cf. Revelation 1.7;

Matthew 24.30). In their LXX form, the latter three passages would not have suited the evangelist's intentions. On three occasions, John expresses the content of an Old Testament passage in his own free rendering, while at the same time presenting the passage as a quotation by using an introductory formula (7.42; 8.17; 12.34). In these cases, it is of course irrelevant to ask which version he used, because the quotation was completely rewritten.

In what follows, I intend to study the text of four Old Testament quotations in the gospel of John. In all four cases my question will be: what changes did the evangelist introduce into his Old Testament text, and why did he make these changes?

John 1.23 = Isaiah 40.3

At the beginning of his narrative (1.19–23), the fourth evangelist says that envoys are sent by the authorities in Jerusalem to ask John the Baptist who he really is: is he the Christ, or the prophet Elijah come back to Earth, or perhaps a prophet like Moses, announced by Moses in Deuteronomy 18.15, 18? John the Baptist answers all these questions in the negative; he claims for himself only a very modest role. When he finally gives a positive account of himself, he identifies himself with the nameless 'voice' from Isaiah 40.3:

> I am the voice of one crying in the wilderness:
> Make straight the way of the Lord,
> as the prophet Isaiah said. (1.23)

The source of this quotation is the LXX:[6]

> The voice of one crying in the wilderness:
> Prepare the way of the Lord,
> make straight the paths of our God.

The LXX has two parallel clauses: 'Prepare the way of the Lord', 'make straight the paths of our God'; John abbreviates these to one clause: 'Make straight the way of the Lord'. He uses it to refers to the testimony the Baptist bears on behalf of Jesus: John the Baptist is the one who makes straight the way of Jesus (1.19–37; 3.23–30). Why did the evangelist change the LXX text in this way? The other evangelists apparently had no problem with the full text; they simply replaced 'the paths of our God' by 'his paths', so that the quotation could be applied to Jesus (Matthew 3.3; Mark 1.3; Luke 3.4).

This question could be answered by assuming that the evangelist was quoting from memory, and made a small error. But this answer is only acceptable for want of something better. In the light of what we know about the familiarity with the scriptures among first-century Jews and Christians and about the ways they treated them, it is an unlikely hypothesis. Until the contrary has been demonstrated, we may assume that the change in the quotation was deliberate.

To my mind, John modified the quotation because in its original form it did not fit into the image he wanted to draw of the relationship between John the Baptist and Jesus. The crux of the matter is the implication of the verb 'prepare' in the clause 'prepare the way of the Lord'. That a person A prepares the way for a person B, in the literal or in the metaphorical sense, often has this connotation: A constructs or repairs the way, and afterwards, once the way is ready, B comes and makes use of it. So, person A appears first on the scene, and it is only after he or she has completed his task that B comes. That John the Baptist prepares the way for Jesus, then, implies that the Baptist appears first, proclaims his message and baptizes, and when he has completed his task Jesus begins his work. This is the way in which the synoptic evangelists present the events: the ministry of John the Baptist ends with the baptism of Jesus, and only after the Baptist has been jailed does Jesus begin his public ministry (Matthew 3.13–17, 4.12; Mark 1.9–11, 14; in Luke 3.19–22, even John's arrest is narrated before the baptism of Jesus). So it is not surprising that the synoptics simply retain the words 'prepare the way of the Lord' in their quotation.

The fourth evangelist presents things in a somewhat different way. As soon as John the Baptist appears on the scene, Jesus is there too. On the first of the two days during which the Baptist testifies to Jesus (1.19–28), the Baptist says about Jesus, 'In the midst of you stands one whom you do not know' (1.26). The next day, he sees Jesus coming towards him and bears witness on his behalf: Jesus is the Lamb of God and the Son of God (1.29–34). Here, the Baptist alludes to Jesus' baptism as a past event (1.32–4). One day later, John the Baptist draws the attention of two of his disciples to Jesus, and they become his first disciples (1.35–7). Later, when Jesus is returning from his first visit to Jerusalem (cf. 2.13, 3.22), John the Baptist is baptizing in the region of Samaria (3.23), and the evangelist remarks explicitly, 'For John had not yet been thrown into prison' (3.24). The Baptist witnesses again on behalf of Jesus (3.27–30).

Apparently, the fourth evangelist wishes to make the ministry of the Baptist contemporaneous with the first part of Jesus' ministry. For him, the Baptist is not so much Jesus' precursor as a witness who appears next to Jesus.

With this presentation of John the Baptist, the evangelist is possibly disputing with a group of disciples of the Baptist who considered their master as the Messiah. On the basis of the principle 'What is earlier is better', they may have claimed that the status of their master was higher than that of Jesus because he preceded Jesus. The existence of this group is a conjecture, but it is one that explains why the fourth evangelist so explicitly denies that John the Baptist is the light or the Messiah (1.8, 20; 3.28; cf. 5.35). It also explains why he makes the ministry of the Baptist simultaneous with that of Jesus and not prior to it.

The evangelist knew of course that the ministry of John the Baptist in fact began before that of Jesus. Indeed, he admits this by having the Baptist refer to Jesus as 'the one who comes after me' (1.15, 27; cf. 1.30), and by making him say of himself, 'I am sent before him' (3.28). However, the evangelist immediately shows the relativity of the Baptist's historical priority by stressing his meta-historical inferiority over against Jesus: 'The one who comes after me ranks before me, because he was earlier than I' (1.15; cf. 1.30). In the prologue, the evangelist brings out the contrast between the eternal being of the Logos and the historical appearance of the man John (1.1, 6).

To the fourth evangelist, John the Baptist is first and foremost a witness alongside Jesus. Therefore he cannot prepare the way for Jesus, but at most make it straight. This view offers an explanation for the change in the quotation from Isaiah 40.3.

John 2.17 = Psalm 69.10

In John 2.13–22, we find the Johannine version of the story of the cleansing of the temple. After Jesus has expelled the merchants from the temple, his disciples remember that it is written, 'Zeal for your house will consume me' (2.17).

John's quotation agrees literally with the translation of the LXX, except for one detail. Instead of John's future tense, the LXX (Psalm 68.10) has a past tense (an aorist indicative in Greek): 'Zeal for your house has consumed me'. There are two LXX manuscripts which, like John, use a future tense here (Codex Vaticanus and Codex Sinaiticus), but their reading can readily be accounted for as an adaptation of the

LXX text to that of John. The textual transmission of the LXX has been for the most part a Christian affair, and in the case of Old Testament passages which are quoted in the New Testament in a form that differs from the LXX, the New Testament passage has often influenced the transmission of the LXX text or vice versa. In the LXX version of the psalm, verses 8–12 contain a continuous series of past tenses (aorist indicatives); it would be very strange indeed if this series were interrupted suddenly by a single future tense. The Hebrew text has a comparable series (perfects and *imperfecta consecutiva*). And when Paul quotes in Romans 15.3 the second half of Psalm 69.10, 'The insults of those who insult you have fallen upon me', he uses an aorist indicative as well.

It is obvious then that it is the fourth evangelist who has interfered with the LXX text by changing a past tense into a future tense. Perhaps he was prompted by the Hebrew text, which uses the Hebrew perfect: this form may have a future meaning, and if one isolates Psalm 69.10a from its context, a translation with a future tense is defensible. The question is: why did John prefer this translation?

One could argue as follows: by this change the evangelist made the psalm passage into a prophecy, an announcement of a future event, and he wants to say here that Jesus' disciples saw the prophecy become reality in Jesus' action in the temple. Zeal for the temple consumes Jesus so much, burns inside him as an inner fire to such an extent, that he drives out the merchants who made God's house into a house of trade. However, this explanation is problematic: if this really is what the evangelist meant to say, the change of tense is unnecessary. John regularly inserts a quotation from scripture at the end of an episode of his story about Jesus' life and death, to demonstrate that the event in question is in agreement with scripture. In such cases, however, the evangelist does not see any problem in maintaining the tense of his source, even if that is a past tense; see 12.38 = Isaiah 53.1; 12.40 = Isaiah 6.10; 13.18 = Psalm 41.10; 15.25 = Psalm 69.5 (or Psalm 35.19); 19.24 = Psalm 22.19. For John, Old Testament passages in the preterite can apparently still constitute prophecies concerning Jesus.

There is a better explanation for the future tense in John 2.17: the quotation means that Jesus' zeal for God's house will cause his death on the cross. The future tense then announces Jesus' death, which still belongs to the future from the perspective of the disciples who are witnessing the cleansing of the temple. This explanation fits in very well with the fact that in early Christianity, the suffering of the righteous one in Psalm 69 was frequently considered as having been realized in Jesus' passion (see, in addition to Romans 15.3, Matthew 27.34, 48; Mark 15.23, 36; Luke 23.36; John 15.25, 19.28; Acts 1.20). It also fits in better with the tenor of Psalm 69.10 within the context of the whole psalm: that zeal consumes the psalmist means that it brings him close to death. Does this explanation also fit in with the Johannine context?

In the pericope of the cleansing of the temple, we hear *twice* about the recollection of the disciples. First, they remember immediately after Jesus' action that it is written in Psalm 69.10 that 'zeal for your house will consume me' (2.17). Next, we hear in 2.22, after Jesus' announcement, in veiled terms, of his resurrection (2.19–21), that after the resurrection his disciples recall that he had said these words, and that they then believe the scripture and Jesus' word. The latter kind of recollection is also discussed elsewhere in John (12.16). It is a recollection that is brought about by the Spirit and that leads to an understanding of Jesus' true significance, which for John is, at the same time, the true significance of scripture (cf. 14.26; 16.13–15; the word 'true' is of course understood here in the Christian sense). In John 2.17, however, the evangelist aims at another, more provisional reminiscence of the scriptural word: it precedes in time the believing reminiscence that grasps the true significance of the scriptural word. The disciples have witnessed Jesus' action in the temple, and at that moment they understand that by his action he antagonizes 'the Jews'. They realize that the conflict arising here may very well cost him his life. They see their expectation confirmed in the words of Psalm 69.10, just as elsewhere in John they express the expectation that events will end badly for their master (11.8, 16; cf. 5.18 etc.). At the same time, the Christian reader of the fourth gospel knows more than the disciples in the story: for this reader, the psalm quotation means that Jesus' death has been announced in scripture and is thus in agreement with God's plan.

So the change in this quotation of a past tense to a future serves to apply the quotation to Jesus' death. The disciples in the story have not yet seen this event in the right perspective, but the informed Christian reader is able to see it that way.

John 12.40 = Isaiah 6.10

In 12.37–43 the fourth evangelist looks back on the reactions evoked by Jesus' public ministry. The result is not spectacular: in spite of the many signs performed by Jesus, 'they did not believe in him'. The evangelist considers this fact to be the fulfilment of Isaiah 53.1: 'Lord, who has believed the report about us,[7] and to whom has the arm of the Lord been revealed?' (12.37–8). He then quotes from Isaiah 6.10 to prove that they could not believe (12.39–40). In John's gospel, this Isaian verse reads – in a literal English translation – as follows:

> He has blinded their eyes,
> and he maimed[8] their heart,
> lest they should see with the eyes,
> and understand with the heart,
> and turn, and I heal them.

The Hebrew text of the verse runs (translated literally):

> Make fat the heart of this people,
> and their ears make heavy,
> and their eyes paste,
> lest they see with their eyes,
> and with their ears hear,
> and their heart understand,
> and they turn, and find healing.

The LXX reads (again in a literal translation):

> For grown fat has the heart of this people,
> and with their ears they have heavily heard,
> and their eyes they have closed,
> lest they see with the eyes,
> and with the ears hear,
> and with the heart understand,
> and turn, and I heal them.

I will now discuss two peculiarities which the Johannine version of Isaiah 6.10 shows in comparison with the Hebrew text and the LXX: the structure of the quotation, and the change of the subject of the clause in the first two lines.

In the Hebrew text and the LXX, the first six lines display a concentric pattern. In the first three lines the prophet speaks of what should happen or has happened to, successively, the heart, the ears and the eyes of the people. In the next three lines he speaks of the intended effect on, successively, the eyes, the ears and the heart. John however modifies the text of Isaiah by omitting the lines about the ears, and by changing the concentric pattern into a parallel pattern: twice in succession he has the prophet first speak of the eyes, and then of the heart, of the people.

What aim is served by this change? The key is to be found just a bit earlier, in 12.37: 'Although he [Jesus] had done so many signs before them, they did not believe in him'. For John, faith is directly related to seeing Jesus' miracles in the right way. According to 2.11, the disciples believe after having witnessed the miracle of water changed into wine in Cana, a sign in which Jesus revealed his glory. Before calling Lazarus from the grave, Jesus prays to his Father 'because of the crowd standing by, that they may believe that you have sent me' (11.42), and seeing the sign of the raising of Lazarus brings many to belief (11.45). The beloved disciple sees the empty tomb and believes (20.8), Thomas sees the risen Lord and believes (20.24–9). The evangelist reports that he has written down a number of Jesus' signs 'that you may believe that Jesus is the Christ, the Son of God' (20.31). Next to this seeing, there is a merely exterior seeing of the signs, which does not, or not yet, lead to real faith (e.g., 2.23–4, 6.14–15). In this connection belongs 12.37: the signs are seen, but faith does not follow. Thus, in the Isaiah quotation, which is brought forward to explain this unbelief, we hear then that God 'has blinded their eyes . . . , lest they should see with the eyes'; this can only mean that God has denied them right seeing.

The heart is often considered the seat of faith (see, e.g., Luke 24.25; Romans 10.8–10); in John, this seems to be the case as well (see 14.1). For the evangelist, then, the second and fourth line of the quotation ('and he maimed their heart . . . and understand with the heart') deal with the incapacity to believe, an incapacity caused by God. The blinding of the eyes brings it about that one cannot perceive the signs in the right way, and the maiming of the heart has the effect that seeing is not followed by faith. John's ideas on the relation of seeing and faith were the motive for his omission of the lines about the ears, and for twice following a line about the eyes with a line about the heart.

Consider now the second peculiarity of the Johannine version of Isaiah 6.10: according to the first two lines, *God* is supposed to have blinded the eyes of the people and maimed their heart. John makes God the cause of unbelief. In the Hebrew text, the prophet receives from God the order to bring the people to deeper unbelief, by way of punishment for the unbelief that is already there: *he* has to make fat the heart of the people, etc. In the LXX, this bold statement is mitigated: now the profound unbelief is an established fact; it is apparently not due to God but to the people themselves. John goes in exactly the opposite direction: he reinforces the tendency that is already latent in the Hebrew text to make God the author of unbelief. The Hebrew text offers him the opportunity to do so: if just a few minor changes are introduced into the vocalization of the Hebrew, the imperatives 'paste' and 'make fat' can be read as forms of the third-person singular of the perfect. In addition, John chooses slightly tendentious Greek translations for the Hebrew verbs, which results in 'he has blinded' and 'he maimed'.

This change is also linked to the theology of the evangelist. He considers both belief and unbelief to be brought about by God, as is evident from Jesus' saying in 6.44: 'No one can come to me unless the Father who sent me draws him' (cf., e.g., 6.37, 64–5; 10.26–9). Of course, such a view raises many theological problems which cannot be discussed here. I confine myself to one remark: in the fourth gospel, deterministic statements like the one just quoted stand alongside other statements which presuppose that human beings are free to believe or not (e.g., 10.37–9; 12.36, 42). Apparently, John does not see a contradiction between belief and unbelief as the work of God and as a human decision.

The drastic changes which the evangelist introduces in Isaiah 6.10 therefore become comprehensible as soon as we connect them to his theology of seeing and believing, and of the origin of belief and unbelief.

John 19.36 = Psalm 34.21 and Exodus 12.46

The fourth evangelist relates in 19.31–7 what happens immediately after Jesus' death. 'The Jews' ask Pilate for the legs of the three condemned men to be broken (to hasten their death), and their bodies to be taken down from the cross before the sabbath (cf. Deuteronomy 21.22–3). Thereupon soldiers come and break the legs of the two who were crucified with Jesus. When they see that Jesus has already died, they do not break his legs. The evangelist sees in this the fulfilment of a word of scripture, which runs in a literal translation: 'Not a bone of him shall be broken'.

Where does this quotation come from? There is no Old Testament passage that agrees exactly with John's quotation; there are however some passages that are rather similar. First of all, there is Exodus 12.46, a regulation concerning the eating of the paschal lamb. It reads, in the

Hebrew text and the LXX, 'You shall not break a bone of it' (the LXX adds the same words in Exodus 12.10). In Numbers 9.12, the regulation is repeated in the third person, in both the Hebrew text and the LXX: 'They shall not break a bone of it'. The striking difference between John and the Torah is that John has a passive verbal form, whereas the regulation in the Torah is in an active form.

There is another Old Testament passage which is also quite similar to the quotation in John 19.36, namely Psalm 34.21. The theme of the last part of Psalm 34 is the salvation of the righteous one by God. In that context, it is said of God in verse 21:

He guards all his bones,
not one of them is broken.

The LXX has here (Psalm 33.21):

The Lord guards all their bones,
not one of them shall be broken.

Here we find exactly the element absent from the regulation concerning the paschal lamb: the passive verbal form. Moreover, the LXX, just like John, puts the verb in the future tense: 'shall be broken'.

It seems that in John's quotation the regulation from the Law and the psalm verse have been treated as analogous passages from scripture. This combination fits very well into the fourth gospel, as we shall now see.

Throughout his gospel, John identifies Jesus with the Old Testament figure of the righteous sufferer who will be vindicated by God. We have already studied the quotation from Psalm 69.10 in 2.17. According to 15.25, Jesus sees in the hatred of the world towards him the fulfilment of Psalm 69.5 (or 35.19): 'They hated me without reason'. When Jesus is hanging on the cross, he says, 'that scripture might be fulfilled', 'I thirst' (19.28). That seems to be an allusion to Psalm 69.22: 'And for my thirst they gave me vinegar to drink'. Judas' betrayal appears to have been announced in the words of Psalm 41.10: 'He who eats my bread has raised his heel against me' (13.18). When the soldiers who have crucified Jesus divide his clothes and draw lots for his tunic, the evangelist sees in this event the fulfilment of Psalm 22.19: 'They divided my garments among them, and for my clothing they cast lots' (19.24). Whether John borrows these quotations from tradition or inserts them himself, he apparently wishes to show that Jesus takes over the role of the righteous sufferer.[9] At the same time, these quotations indirectly announce the resurrection: in all of the psalms just mentioned, the salvation of the righteous one is also a theme.

In addition to this, the fourth evangelist describes Jesus as the true paschal lamb. He does not do so directly, but by means of his chronology. Unlike the synoptics, John does not explicitly characterize Jesus' last meal with his disciples as a Passover meal, and according to John, Jesus does not die on the first day of Passover, but on the afternoon of the day before. The last meal takes place 'before the feast of Passover' (13.1); at the moment Jesus is brought to Pilate, the Passover meal has yet to be eaten (18.28), and Jesus appears before Pilate on the day of preparation before Passover, around noon (19.14). This means that Jesus is hanging on the cross at the same time as the paschal lambs are being slaughtered in the temple. The evangelist thus suggests that Jesus is the true paschal lamb, slaughtered on the cross (a thought which is already found in Paul; see 1 Corinthians 5.7). John's quotation, which incorporates the regulation that the bones of the paschal lamb should not be broken, shows the same typology.

So two qualifications of Jesus, both stemming from the Old Testament, meet in the quotation of 19.36: he is the righteous sufferer and the true paschal lamb. In this respect, the quotation is typical of the christology of the fourth evangelist: in John's view, all possible titles and indications that characterize the eschatological saviour should be applied to Jesus (see, e.g., the series of christological titles in 1.1–51).

Conclusion

On the basis of four examples, we have seen how the fourth evangelist edits and interprets quotations from scripture. He changes a word, shortens and omits lines of verse, and combines passages. I would like to emphasize that these adaptations remain within the boundaries of what was regarded as acceptable in Judaism and Christianity around the end of the first century. He does not work arbitrarily, but in a well-thought-out way.

In all four examples, his motive for the changes is the same: the wish to make the quotations applicable to what he wants to say to his hearers or readers about Jesus and his significance. His interpretation of scripture is determined by his view of Jesus. On the basis of his belief in Jesus as the Christ, the Son of God, he searches for a legitimation of this belief, in the interest of his fellow-believers and of himself.

Undoubtedly Jews in the environment of the evangelist and his community interpreted the same scriptures quite differently, and in the conflict between the Johannine community and their Jewish environment both parties were ready to resort to scripture when disputing with each other (see John 5.37–47). Apparently, the Old Testament could be read in more than one way: Christians read it as testimony on behalf of Jesus, Jews as testimony against him. One cannot assert that the Old Testament points to Jesus objectively and unambiguously; Jewish and Christian convictions also determine the way it is read. In the past, the interpretation of the Old Testament functioned mainly as a point of contention in confrontations between Jews and Christians. In the current dialogue between Jews and Christians, both parties have fortunately become more and more aware that the scriptures, which Christians call the Old Testament, are also a common point of departure.[10]

Notes

1 See G. Reim, *Studien zum alttestamentlichen Hintergrund des Johannesevangeliums* (SNTSMS 22), Cambridge: Cambridge University Press, 1974, pp. 97–205; A. T. Hanson, *The Prophetic Gospel: A Study of John and the Old Testament* (Edinburgh: T & T Clark, 1991); U. Busse, 'Die Tempelmetaphorik als ein Beispiel von implizitem Rekurs auf die biblische Tradition im Johannesevangelium', in C. M. Tuckett (ed.), *The Scriptures in the Gospels* (BETL 131), Leuven: Leuven University/Peeters, 1997, pp. 395–428; M. Daly-Denton, *David in the Fourth Gospel: The Johannine Reception of the Psalms* (AGJU 47); Leiden: Brill, 2000, pp. 243–315.

2 See E. D. Freed, *Old Testament Quotations in the Gospel of John* (NovT Sup. 11), Leiden: Brill, 1965; Reim, *Studien*, pp. 1–96; B. G. Schuchard, *Scripture within Scripture: The Interrelationship of Form and Function in the Explicit Old Testament Citations in the Gospel of John* (SBLDS 133), Atlanta: Scholars Press, 1992); M. J. J. Menken, *Old Testament Quotations in the Fourth Gospel: Studies in Textual Form* (CBET 15), Kampen: Kok Pharos, 1996; M. J. J. Menken, 'The Use of the Septuagint in Three Quotations in John: Jn 10:34; 12:38; 19:24', in Tuckett (ed.), *The Scriptures in the Gospels*, pp. 367–93; A. Obermann, *Die christologische Erfüllung der Schrift im Johannesevangelium: Eine Untersuchung zur johanneischen Hermeneutik anhand der Schriftzitate* (WUNT 2.82), Tübingen: Mohr, 1996; Daly-Denton, *David in the Fourth Gospel*, pp.115–242.

3 See C. H. Dodd, *According to the Scriptures: The Sub-structure of New Testament Theology*, London: Nisbet, 1952; B. Lindars, *New Testament Apologetic: The Doctrinal Significance of the Old Testament Quotations*, London: SCM, 1961.

4 This observation is clearly also valid, *mutatis mutandis*, for other New Testament authors.
5 See J. Koenig, *L'herméneutique analogique du Judaïsme antique d'après les témoins textuels d'Isaïe* (VTSup 33, Leiden: Brill, 1982; also G. J. Brooke, *Exegesis at Qumran: 4QFlorilegium in its Jewish Context* (JSOTSup 29), Sheffield: JSOT, 1985.
6 Possibly a revised LXX: see Menken, *Old Testament Quotations*, pp. 24–5.
7 For this translation, see Menken, 'Use of the Septuagint', pp. 384–6.
8 On the Greek text underlying this translation, see Menken, *Old Testament Quotations*, pp. 101–4.
9 It will be clear that the Johannine Jesus does not *completely* identify with the righteous sufferer: the righteous sufferer feels abandoned by God (Psalm 22.2), but John presents Jesus as being in permanent intimate communication with his Father (John 16.32). Typology is always selective.
10 I thank John M. Court for improving the English of this essay.

5

'Who Has Believed Our Message?': Paul's Reading of Isaiah

Richard B. Hays

I. Introduction

How did Paul read Isaiah? The question has usually not been posed in just this way. Most New Testament scholars have tended to assume that Paul merely exploited the Old Testament as a collection of oracular proof-texts, without regard for original context; thus, the idea that Paul read any individual Old Testament book as a literary or theological unity has seldom, if ever, been entertained. A careful examination of the evidence, however, might lead to different, and interesting, conclusions.

Paul seems to have had a special interest in Isaiah. In the seven letters generally acknowledged as authentic, Paul quotes Isaiah 31 times (out of an approximate total of 89 Old Testament quotations overall in these letters).[1] Furthermore, in his letter to the Romans, Paul cites Isaiah explicitly by name five times (Romans 9.27, 29; 10.16, 20; 15.12). It is noteworthy that, while the 31 quotations are taken from throughout the book of Isaiah, there are significant clusters of citations from some sections, notably chapters 28–9 (six quotations) and 49–55 (ten quotations). The evidence is even more impressive if we count allusions as well as explicit quotations. Allusions are more difficult to quantify precisely, but the list given in Nestle–Aland (27th edn) can serve as a rough indicator: out of 50 allusions to Isaiah in the seven-letter corpus, 21 of them point to Isaiah 49–55. (Paul was of course innocent of the modern critical division of Isaiah into three parts, but he seems to have been drawn particularly to the section of the book that modern scholarship has designated as Deutero-Isaiah.)

This chapter was first published in the *Society of Biblical Literature 1998 Seminar Papers*, pp. 205–24.

This rough statistical evidence suggests – at the very least – that Paul attributed particular significance to the prophecies of Isaiah, and that he found some portions of this prophetic book to be particularly useful in his interpretation and defence of the gospel. The reasons for this are not difficult to fathom. Isaiah, more clearly than any other Old Testament book, links the promise of the redemption and restoration of Israel to the hope that Israel's God will also reveal his mercy to the Gentiles and establish sovereignty over the whole earth. Thus, Paul finds in Isaiah – particularly the prophecies of Deutero-Isaiah – a prefiguration of his own distinctive apostolic ministry to the Gentiles.[2]

Christian interpreters of the New Testament have sometimes focused on the depiction of the 'Suffering Servant' of Isaiah 53 as a key to Pauline christology (although this approach was dealt a severe blow by Morna Hooker's monograph of forty years ago, *Jesus and the Servant*[3]). It is possible that Paul may have read Isaiah 53 as a prophecy of Christ's vicarious suffering, but it is hard to substantiate this claim. I believe, however, that Paul's explicit use of Isaiah is uncontestably 'ecclesiocentric', as is his use of scripture more generally.[4] His reading of Isaiah points primarily towards the formation of an eschatological people of God in which Gentiles are to be included. Indeed, he seems to find in Isaiah not only a *warrant* for his apostolic ministry to Gentiles but also a direct prophetic *prediction* of it, closely analogous to the way in which the Qumran covenanters read scriptural texts as prophecies of their own communal life and vocation.

Once this insight is established through attention to Paul's explicit quotations of Isaiah, I believe that we may discern the broader outlines of Paul's overall reading of the book. The explicit citations are merely the tip of the iceberg; they point to a larger mass just under the surface, Paul's comprehensive construal of Isaiah as a coherent witness to the gospel.[5] I believe that Paul had read and pondered the scroll of Isaiah as a whole, over the years of his apostolic ministry, and developed a sustained reading of it as God's revelation of 'the mystery that was kept secret for long ages but is now disclosed, and through the prophetic writings is made known to all the Gentiles, according to the command of the eternal God, to bring about the obedience of faith' (Romans 16.25–6).[6] In order to make this claim credible, however, I must digress to examine the model of reading that I bring to my task. Paul's reading of Isaiah is just one instance of the larger phenomenon of intertextual reading and writing by early Christian authors. Thus, some slightly broader methodological reflection is required.

II. Reading Intertextually: A Literary-Theological Paradigm

If we want to understand what the New Testament writers were doing theologically – particularly how they interpreted the relation of the gospel to the more ancient story of God's covenant relationship to Israel – we cannot avoid the effort to trace and understand their hermeneutical appropriation of Israel's scriptures. This is so *a fortiori* for Paul, the self-described Hebrew of Hebrews who, by his own account, surpassed all his contemporaries in zeal for the traditions of his fathers. He received and passed on – indeed, insisted upon – the tradition that the death and resurrection of Jesus had happened κατὰ τὰς γραφὰς (1 Corinthians 15.3), and he persistently developed his theological arguments in relation to the stories and oracles that he found in those scriptures. His letter to the Romans opens with the affirmation that 'the gospel of God' was 'promised ahead of time through his prophets in holy writings' (Romans 1.2),[7] and in the course of his argument in this letter he quotes scripture more than sixty times.[8] Despite the puzzling resistance of some New Testament scholarship to acknowledging the formative role of the Old Testament in Paul's theology,[9] it must be affirmed that Paul was a hermeneutical theologian whose reflection on God's action in the world was shaped in decisive ways by his reading of Israel's sacred texts.[10]

It would, therefore, be highly artificial to suppose that scripture plays an important role in Paul's thought only in those cases where he quotes a text explicitly. There can be no serious doubt that scripture shapes his symbolic world in a more pervasive manner.[11] That means that our efforts to interpret his writings must deal also with allusions and echoes of scripture in his writings.

Some of these allusions and echoes may have been deliberately crafted by the Apostle, presupposing recognition from Christian readers in the Pauline communities whom Paul himself had explicitly trained to understand certain scriptural motifs. Others may be less deliberate, simply bubbling up out of Paul's mind in the same way that allusions to Shakespeare or Milton might arise unbidden for any English writer educated in the English literary tradition – or, let us say, allusions to Luther or Goethe for the German writer. From this distance in time, however, it is difficult to distinguish between intentional and unintentional intertextual references in Paul. Because the question of authorial intentionality is a slippery one, we should not place too much weight upon it; for the present let us simply say that to interpret Paul discerningly we must recognize the embeddedness of his discourse in scriptural language (or the embeddedness of scriptural language in his discourse) and explore the rhetorical and theological effects created by the intertextual relationships between his letters and their scriptural precursors.

Identifying allusions and echoes of an earlier text in a later one, however, poses a daunting challenge, especially when we encounter texts that come to us from the ancient world. Thomas Greene, a literary scholar who has studied the use of classical sources in Renaissance literature, describes the difficulty of this sort of intertextual reading:

> [It] makes even larger claims on the historical imagination than most reading, and underscores even more cruelly our cultural solitude. It asks us not only to intuit an alien sensibility from a remote *mundus significans*, but also that sensibility's intuitions of a third. Nothing perhaps is more calculated to impress upon us our temporal estrangement.[12]

Thus, this sort of interpretative task calls for close attention and discernment on the part of the reader: or, more precisely, on the part of the reading community. The danger of rampant subjectivity and misinterpretation is very great.

Consequently, we must consider how we, as a community of trained and presumably competent readers, shall discipline our intuitions about the role of scripture in Paul's *mundus significans*. If the identification of allusions and echoes in Paul is not to be a purely private romp through infinite fields of intertextual possibility, what are the *criteria* that might be applied to test our hunches about Paul's indirect literary gestures towards the Old Testament, particularly towards Isaiah?

I have some proposals to make about the criteria we might use, but before stating my positive criteria, I want to voice three preliminary cautions and clarifications about this enterprise, in hopes of heading off certain confusions.

1. Paul had no conception of 'the Servant Songs' as a distinct collection or genre within the Isaianic prophetic material. The idea of a cycle of Servant Songs is a construct of modern critical scholarship. Our tendency to focus especially on the Servant material, a tendency which arises partly from the way the texts were later used in the construction of christology and partly from the development of form-critical methods for studying the Old Testament, may create a distortion of perspective. Paul seems to have used the Isaiah material in an undifferentiated

manner, without paying any special attention to the passages about the Servant, though, as we have noted, he does cite and allude to Isaiah 40—55 with particular frequency. Thus, rather than asking, at least in the first instance, 'How did Paul interpret the figure of the Servant in Isaiah 53?', we should begin by observing inductively how Paul employs the Isaiah material more generally.

2. The identification of allusions and especially of echoes is not a strictly scientific matter lending itself to conclusive proof, like testing for the presence or absence of a chemical in the bloodstream. The identification of allusions, rather, is an art practised by skilled interpreters within a reading community that has agreed on the value of situating individual texts within a historical and literary continuum of other texts (i.e., a canon). The 'yes' or 'no' judgement about any particular alleged allusion is primarily an *aesthetic* judgement pronounced upon the fittingness of a proposed reading. This does *not* mean, I hasten to add, that such judgements are purely arbitrary, any more than judgements about the quality of a particular performance of a Mozart piano concerto are arbitrary; there are norms and standards internal to the practice, and those who have studied the practice closely should be able to develop significantly convergent judgements. The ability to recognize – or to exclude – possible allusions is a skill, a reader competence, inculcated by reading communities.

3. Finally, we must consider the aims of the interpretative task we are undertaking. Are we trying to prove a historical hypothesis about Isaiah's direct influence on the early Church's development of the idea that Jesus' death had atoning significance? Or, alternatively, are we trying to understand the way in which an author (Paul) creates meaning effects in a text through artful reminiscences of another text well known to the community? These are very different tasks: the former is primarily historical, the latter literary and theological. Both are perfectly legitimate pursuits – indeed, they are methodologically intertwined – but it is important to be clear about where the focus of our attention lies.

Much of the debate about the use of Isaiah in the New Testament has dealt with the historical issues. Consider, by way of illustration, the following quotation from Hooker, in which I have underlined the phrases that indicate her concentration on proving historical claims about Isaiah 53 as the unique source of christological ideas:

> No attempt to <u>resolve the dilemma</u> on linguistic grounds alone can be successful if the <u>evidence</u> is only <u>probable</u>. To claim that there is a verbal

similarity between a New Testament passage and an Old Testament one cannot be taken as <u>conclusive evidence</u> of <u>direct influence</u> unless it can be shown that the language and ideas found in the New Testament reference have come from, *and could only have come from*, that particular Old Testament passage. Unless the New Testament passage is an actual quotation from the Old Testament, or contains an idea found <u>uniquely</u> in that Old Testament reference, then the claim remains only as subsidiary <u>evidence</u>, and cannot be accepted as <u>proof</u> of any identification.[13]

In the nature of the case, of course, it is difficult to *prove* things about sources and direct influences, given the paucity of evidence at our disposal. That is one reason why Hooker's book had such an impact on the discussion in the English-speaking world: given her stringent criteria for proof, her arguments seemed nearly irrefutable. Indeed, the book served the important purpose of clearing away a lot of wild and undisciplined claims about the Servant image; particularly valuable was her demonstration that Jews in the first century CE were not looking for a Messiah to fulfil the Suffering Servant role.

More recent scholarship, however, has begun to articulate a different paradigm for thinking about intertextual relations. My own work on Paul's use of scripture has sought to explore in the epistles what John Ciardi called the 'rippling pools' of metaphor and allusion, and other interpreters have become more attuned to the rhetorical effects within the Pauline texts. In point of fact, such approaches may also contribute to the formation of judgements about historical questions: for example, if we develop a reading of Romans that discovers an extensive network of allusions to Deutero-Isaiah, that will enhance the likelihood (but not 'prove') that Isaiah 53 is one of the significant sources for Paul's interpretation of Jesus. But the primary interest of such readings lies elsewhere, in the literary and theological implications of observable intertextual linkages.

To clarify what I mean by speaking of a different paradigm, let us consider one non-scriptural example, an example not freighted with the theological baggage of past debates in our guild.[14] Near the end of the 'Fire Sermon' section of *The Waste Land*, a section of the poem that vividly depicts the decaying, lustful, and meaningless condition of life in twentieth-century London, T. S. Eliot abruptly writes:

To Carthage then I came

Burning burning burning burning
O Lord Thou pluckest me out
O Lord Thou pluckest

burning

This looks like a random and puzzling series of lines: Why Carthage? What has this to do with London or the decay of modern life? The lines are puzzling, that is, unless we recognize the allusion to the opening of Book III of St Augustine's *Confessions*: 'To Carthage then I came, where a cauldron of unholy loves sang all about mine ears.' With this connection made, Eliot's deft allusion conjures up Augustine's image of the corrupt city and his own immersion in it. Augustine's Carthage becomes a metaphor for Eliot's London, and the 'burning' language – initially borrowed by Eliot from the Buddhist Fire Sermon's aversion to the world of the senses – becomes identified, on at least one level, with the burning of the youthful lusts that Augustine retrospectively deplores. (On another level, 'burning' is also probably a figure for judgement and destruction, the reduction of the city to rubble; the two levels are intimately connected.) The line 'O Lord Thou pluckest me out' should also then be recognized as an allusion to *Confessions* III.xi: 'Et misisti manum tuam ex alto, et de hac profunda caligne eruisti animam meam.'[15] The fact, however, that Eliot's affirmation trails off and collapses back into 'burning' at the end of the passage marks the distance between the Bishop of Hippo and the desolate modern poet: Augustine's confident cry of gratitude to God has become for the speaking persona of *The Waste Land* only a forlorn hope.

Beyond all this, we may note one more nearly subliminal but intriguing echo created by Eliot's allusion to Augustine. The final sentence of *Confessions* II.x, the line just *preceding* 'To Carthage then I came', reads as follows: 'I sank away from Thee, and I wandered, O my God, too much astray from Thee my stay, in these days of my youth, and I became to myself *a barren land*.' This is an elegant and tantalizing example of metalepsis, the suggested but unspoken evocation of an image from the precursor text, echoing in the Waste Land of the latter.

The purpose of this excursus into the world of twentieth-century English poetry has been to illustrate something about the way that allusion and echo work as *tropes*, figurative modes of speech whose efficacy depends partly upon their initial obscurity. We do not make much progress in reading such figures if we confine our enquiry to asking questions like, 'Is Eliot's line an allusion to Augustine, yes or no?' and 'Can we prove that the *Confessions* was a source for *The Waste Land*?' (I'm afraid that many readers trained in the usual methods of biblical studies might insist that Eliot intended no reference to the 'cauldron of unholy loves', because he did not actually quote that part of the line!) We attain an illuminating reading of Eliot's text only when we follow the play of allusion and see where it leads. In the previous paragraphs, I have sketched briefly one such reading of the intertextual figuration.

That is the sort of reading that also yields, I believe, considerable fruit when employed in relation to Paul's letters. Let us turn, then, to consider some criteria for evaluating alleged allusions and echoes.

III. The Seven Criteria of Echoes Applied to Paul's Use of Isaiah

In *Echoes of Scripture in the Letters of Paul* I proposed seven tests for discerning the presence of intertextual echoes in Paul.[16] As I have already indicated, precision in such matters is not attainable, but these are – it still seems to me – modestly useful rules of thumb. For our present purposes, I will restate and elaborate them, with particular application to the question about Paul's reading of Isaiah. It should be kept in mind that no one of these criteria is decisive: they must be employed in conjunction with one another. We should also bear in mind that the use of such criteria will often yield only greater or lesser degrees of probability about any particular reading, especially where echoes are concerned.

Availability
Was the proposed source of the echo available to Paul and/or his original readers? In the case of Isaiah, there can be no doubt about this. Isaiah was broadly recognized as scripture in the Judaism of Paul's time, and Paul quotes it as such repeatedly, using explicit citation formulas, such as λέγει γὰρ ἡ γράφη (Romans 10.11), γέγραπται γὰρ (Romans 14.11), καθὼς γέγραπται (Romans 2.24, 9.33, 10.15, 11.26, 15.21), ἐν τῷ νόμῳ[!] γέγραπται ὅτι (1 Corinthians 14.21), and a series of formulae that mention Isaiah by name: Ἡσαΐας δὲ κράζει ὑπὲρ τοῦ Ἰσραήλ (Romans 9.27), καθὼς προείρηκεν Ἡσαΐας (Romans 9.29), Ἡσαΐας γὰρ λέγει (Romans 10.16), Ἡσαΐας δὲ ἀποτολμᾷ καὶ λέγει (Romans 10.21), and καὶ πάλιν Ἡσαΐας λέγει

(Romans 15.12). Paul certainly knew Isaiah and cited it frequently. His interpretations of the text may have been controversial, but he expected his readers to recognize the source of his quotations and acknowledge it as scripture.

Volume

How 'loud' is the echo: that is, how explicit and overt is it? Of the seven tests suggested in *Echoes*, this one has been perhaps the most subject to misunderstanding, because I did not explain it very fully there. The general notion of the variable 'volume' of echoes is derived from the richly suggestive work of John Hollander, whose book *The Figure of Echo* was a major stimulus to my work on echoes in Paul.[17] The basic question here is how insistently the echo presses itself upon the reader. Let me try to unpack the elements that are involved in assessing this issue.

1. The primary factor is *the degree of verbatim repetition of words and syntactical patterns*. For example, in Romans 8.32 (ὅς γε τοῦ ἰδίου υἱοῦ αὐτοῦ ἐφείσατο), the words 'did not spare his own son' can be heard as an echo of Genesis 22.16 because the words 'son' and 'did not spare' reproduce the language of the Septuagint (LXX) closely. The whole expression, however, has been transferred from the second person to the third, and the subject of the verb in Romans is God rather than, as in Genesis, Abraham. Thus, the volume of this echo is only moderate, and interpreters have long been divided on how to assess its significance or even whether to hear it as an echo at all. To take another example, a much louder echo is to be found in Romans 8.33-4, where we have not only the language of judgement (Isaiah 50.8: τίς ὁ κρινόμενός μοι;/ Romans 8.34: τίς ὁ κατακρινῶν;) and God's vindication of the elect (Isaiah 50.8: ἐγγίζει ὁ δικαιώσας με/Romans 8.33: θεὸς ὁ δικαιῶν), but even the same syntactical pattern of brief diatribal rhetorical questions in both texts. Here the echo is very loud indeed; only the most stubborn or tone-deaf reader would deny its presence in Paul's text. To give an example at the other end of the decibel spectrum however, consider this: should Paul's use of the term καινὴ κτίσις (2 Corinthians 5.17, Galatians 6.15) be understood as an allusion to/echo of Isaiah 43.18-19 and/or 65.17? I would argue that it should be so understood, because the echo meets several other important criteria, particularly the criterion of thematic coherence (see below), but the *volume* of the echo – in terms of verbatim repetition of Isaiah's language – is low: it is only the word pair ἀρχαῖα/καινή (hardly an unusual juxtaposition) that appears in both texts.[18]

Of course, to speak of 'verbatim repetition' presumes that we know what text form of the scriptural passages was available to Paul and his readers. This is, unfortunately, a complex technical problem that admits few certain answers.[19] It has been established that Paul's quotations of the Old Testament generally follow the LXX against the Masoretic Text where the two are divergent. Thus, our normal procedure should be to compare alleged scriptural allusions in Paul first of all to the LXX, as I have done in the examples cited in the previous paragraph. If in some instances evidence from later Greek versions agrees with Paul's wording against the LXX, this opens the possibility that Paul may be echoing a Greek text – presumably known to his readers – that differs from extant LXX manuscripts, or that he is modifying the LXX in accord with common linguistic usage of his own day.[20] Sometimes scholars claim to hear in Paul's letters echoes or allusions of an underlying Hebrew or Aramaic text that differs from any of the Greek versions; such proposals are not impossible (my own view is that Paul surely must have known Hebrew), but they will always remain speculative,[21] enjoying a lower degree of probability than alleged echoes of a Greek textual source. Most of Paul's readers surely did not know Hebrew or Aramaic; therefore, any echoes of such linguistic origin would have fallen on deaf ears.

2. 'Volume' also depends, however, on *the distinctiveness, prominence, or popular familiarity of the precursor text*. For example, in 1 Corinthians 8.6, Paul's confessional formula echoes Deuteronomy 6.4: 'for us there is *one God*, the Father, . . . and *one Lord*, Jesus Christ. . . .'. Even though the number of words repeated from Deuteronomy is small, the *Shema* is such a familiar and foundational text within Judaism that only a slight verbal cue is needed to trigger the full-volume echo. For an analogy, we might consider how the simple words 'Our Father' will serve to conjure up the entire text of the Lord's Prayer for any Christian reader.[22] American readers might compare the way in which any passing reference to 'self-evident truths' is likely to be heard as an echo of the Declaration of Independence, or the way in which the simple phrase 'I have a dream' can no longer be uttered without echoes of Martin Luther King, Jr. being heard in the background.

3. Finally, the volume of an echo is affected subtly by the rhetorical stress placed upon the phrase(s) in question, both within the precursor text and in Paul's discourse. This is more difficult to illustrate concisely, but I have in mind the recurrence of language that comes from keynote or summary passages in the source text, or language that is placed at a climactic (clinching) point in Paul's own discourse. The

echo of Genesis 1.3–5 in 2 Corinthians 4.6 is an example of this sort of thing.[23]

In short, when we speak of the *volume* of an echo, we must consider not only the degree of exact verbal correspondence, but also the relative weightiness of the material cited.

Recurrence or clustering

How often does Paul elsewhere cite or allude to the same scriptural passage? We might also call this 'multiple attestation'. This criterion is a very important one indeed, and it will play a crucial role in our consideration of echoes of Isaiah in Paul. Authors tend to work with a de facto canon within the canon, certain texts that are more important, more frequently read and adduced. Paul is no exception: there are several instances of passages that he seems to have mulled over at some length. *When we find repeated Pauline quotations of a particular Old Testament passage, additional possible allusions to the same passage become more compelling.* I use the term 'passage' broadly to indicate not just a particular verse quoted explicitly on more than one occasion (such as Habakkuk 2.4 or Genesis 15.6) but also larger units of scripture to which Paul repeatedly refers. One example of this would be Deuteronomy 32, which turns up repeatedly in Paul's letters (e.g., explicit quotations in Romans 10.19, 12.19, 15.10 and clear allusions in 1 Corinthians 10.20, 22 and Romans 11.11).[24] The parade example of this phenomenon in the Pauline letters, however, is his use of Isaiah 40—55.[25] Paul returns again and again to this text, especially in Romans. Here we find clear evidence of the *clustering* of citations from one special scriptural context. Figure 5.1 graphically displays the data concerning Paul's direct quotations of Isaiah in Romans.[26] The evidence is even more impressive if we include allusions in our purview: according to the table of 'Loci citati vel allegati' in Nestle–Aland (27th edn), there are, by my count, 14 quotations from Isaiah 40—55 in the Pauline letters[27] (seven of them appearing in Romans) and 26 more allusions, for a total of 40 references in all. I suspect that this tabulation only scratches the surface of the intertextual networking between Paul and Deutero-Isaiah. In any case, no matter how we might tabulate the precise extent or number of allusions, it is difficult to avoid the impression that Paul was deeply engaged in reflection about this particular passage of scripture.

Of course, it is in principle possible that Paul merely treated Isaiah 40—55 as a loose anthology of favourite religious quotations, without

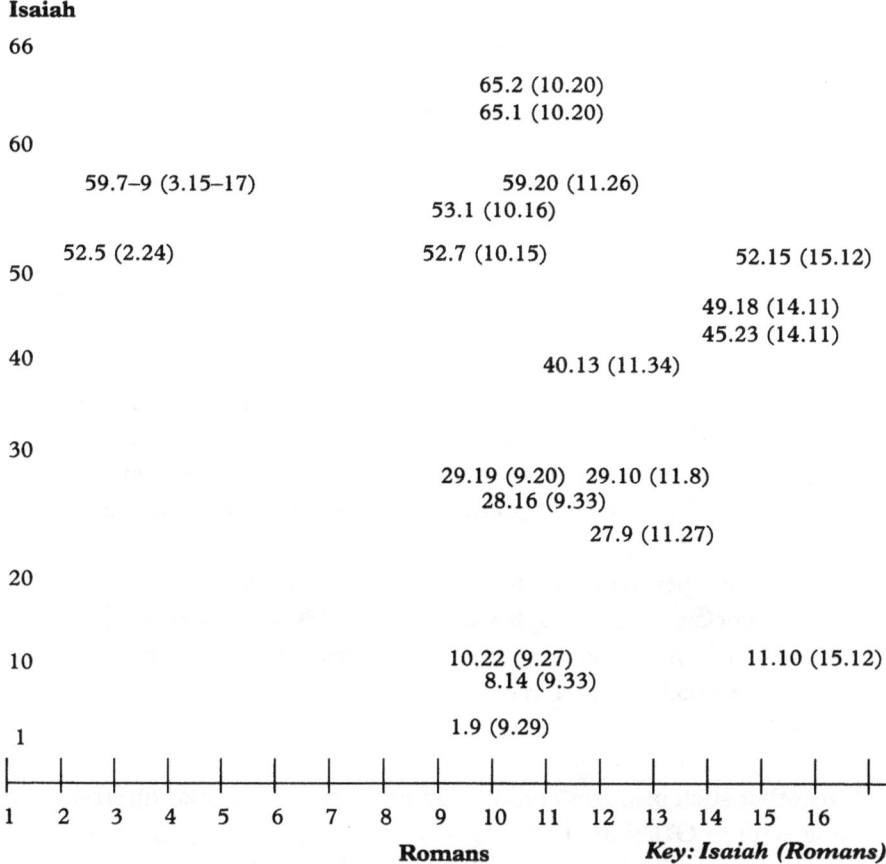

Figure 5.1   Explicit citations of Isaiah in Romans

considering its overall meaning; readers will have to form their own judgement on this point. Even if that were so, however, the criterion of recurrence would still be useful for identifying the *presence* of allusions to Isaiah. The question of the *meaning* of such allusions, however, leads us on to the next criterion.

Thematic Coherence

How well does the alleged echo fit into the line of argument that Paul is developing? Does the proposed precursor text fit together with the point Paul is making? Can one see in Paul's use of the material a coherent 'reading' of the source text? Is his use of the Isaiah texts consonant with his overall argument and/or use made of other texts? Of course, it is perfectly possible for random isolated echoes to occur that do not contribute coherently to the argument, but it would be difficult to test intuitions about such echoes with much confidence. When, however, an echo does fit into a larger thematic pattern, we may more securely identify it.

In fact, when we assemble the evidence, it is possible to mount a strong argument that Paul is not just randomly proof-texting in his allusions to Isaiah but that Isaiah 40—55 is fundamentally formative for his understanding of what God is doing in the world through the proclamation of the gospel: God is revealing his eschatological righteousness, ending the exile of his people, and bringing the Gentiles to see and understand (Romans 15.21, citing Isaiah 52.15). Furthermore, as J. Ross Wagner has shown in his essay 'The Heralds of Isaiah and the Mission of Paul', Paul 'finds in Isaiah a prefiguration or pre-announcement of his own proclamation of the Gospel to Jew and Gentile alike, wherever Christ is not yet known.'[28] Consider, for example, in Romans 10.14–16, the way that Paul cites Isaiah 52.7 and 53.1 as prefigurations of his own preaching activity:

> And how are they to hear without someone to proclaim him? And how are they to proclaim him unless they are sent? As it is written, 'How beautiful are the feet of those who bring good news!' [Isaiah 52.7][29] But not all have obeyed the good news; for Isaiah says, 'Lord, who has believed our message?' [Isaiah 53.1][30]

Many other such passages could be adduced. (Of particular interest is the strong echo in Galatians 1.15 of Isaiah 49.1, suggesting that Paul understood his own 'call' as the fulfilment – or at least the typological counterpart – of the Servant's vocation to be a 'light to the nations', and [perhaps thereby?] to bring Jacob back to the Lord; cf. Isaiah 49.5–6.) The point is that there is abundant evidence in Paul's letters that he read Isaiah 40—55 as a coherent prophetic vision foretelling and authorizing Paul's own apostolic activity. The surprising disclosure of God's righteousness, the proclaiming of the word to the nations, the unbelief of Israel, the apostle's commission to announce the good news of salvation – all these themes are richly suggested by the passages in Isaiah that Paul quotes and echoes. (See the summary in Section IV below, pp. 62ff.) Where we see evidence of Paul's sustained and reflectively patterned reading of a particular text, we may assume that other possible echoes of that same text elsewhere in the same letter are likely to be theologically significant rather than merely the product of our own interpretive fantasy.

Although Hooker's early study of the Servant denies a thematic link between Isaiah 52—3 and Pauline christology, her actual interpretation of the material is convergent with the point I am making here: 'there is a consistent interpretation of the "Servant" which stretches from Deutero-Isaiah, through Judaism, to Jesus himself [and, I would add, to Paul as well]: an interpretation which arises, not from the concept of the "Servant", but from the thought of the mission of people of God to the world.'[31] If indeed that is how Isaiah 52—3 was understood in the Judaism of Paul's day, then is it not credible to find allusions to this text in Paul's theological reflection upon his own mission?

Historical plausibility

Could Paul in fact have intended the alleged meaning-effect of any proposed allusion, and could his first-century readers have understood it? The criterion of historical plausibility requires that the historical situatedness of Paul's letters, as acts of communication, be taken seriously. Paul was a Pharisaic Jew and also a member of the early Christian movement; consequently, he was the heir of certain interpretative traditions within both of these communities. At the same time, he was seeking to mediate to predominantly Gentile readers the meaning of Israel's scripture in the new eschatological situation. In such a situation, and against such a background, what sorts of allusions and echoes would make sense? Here there is much room – indeed, great need – for further research and reflection. How did other Jews in Paul's time read Isaiah? How are his readings like and unlike theirs? What use was made of Isaiah's prophecies in other early Christian interpretations? Can we find parallels to Paul's readings?

This criterion should not necessarily function as a negative constraint, because Paul was no doubt a reasonably original thinker who was capable of formulating fresh echoes and unprecedented readings. Furthermore, many of his more subtle allusions might have eluded his Gentile readers. If, however, it can be shown that Paul's allusions to Scripture do have analogies and parallels in other contemporary writings, then we are on firmer ground in placing interpretative weight upon them. For example, should Paul's strange gloss (ὅς ἐστιν Χριστός) in Galatians 3.16 on the promise to Abraham and to his 'seed' (σπέρματι) be understood as a covert allusion to 2 Samuel 7.12–14, in which God promises to 'raise up' a 'seed' (σπέρμα) of David and 'establish the throne of his kingdom for ever'? This suggestion is made more plausible by the discovery that 4Q Florilegium 1.10–11 includes 2 Samuel 7.12–14 in an anthology of messianic texts.[32] Or again, Paul's strange christological interpretation of Deuteronomy 30.12–14 in Romans

10.6–8 is rendered more comprehensible in light of Baruch 3.29–30, which had already transferred Deuteronomy's language about the Torah onto the personified figure of Wisdom:

> Who has gone up into heaven and taken her,
>   and brought her down from the clouds?
> Who has gone over the sea and found her,
>   and will buy her for pure gold?[33]

The use of this criterion requires of us a broad historical construction of the hermeneutical horizon and reader-competence of Paul and his first-century readers. I am not aware of a recent scholarly monograph thoroughly surveying interpretations of Deutero-Isaiah in the Second Temple period,[34] but some such study would be of great help in our efforts to identify and interpret Pauline allusions to Isaiah.

History of Interpretation

If the previous criterion attends to readings of scripture contemporary with Paul, this one attends to the subsequent history of the reading of Paul's epistles. Have other readers in the tradition heard the same echoes that we now think we hear? Or can the history of interpretation alert us to echoes that we might otherwise have missed?

Again, this criterion may serve more to expand than to veto our intuitions about particular echoes. The Christian tradition early on lost its vital connection with the Jewish interpretive matrix in which Paul had lived and moved; consequently, later Christian interpreters missed some of Paul's basic concerns. For example, the Christian fixation on christological proof-texts may have caused readers to zero in on texts like Isaiah 53 and to overlook Paul's concern for explaining the mission to the Gentiles and the fate of Israel in relation to scripture. This tendency, in turn, may have caused most readers to lose sight of the ecclesiocentric hermeneutic operative in Paul's larger pattern of allusions to Isaiah.[35] Thus, the tradition of interpretation has its blind (or deaf) spots. Traditional readings will need to be supplemented by new readings that benefit from a scholarly recovery of the 'cave of resonant signification' within which Paul's voice originally sounded.[36]

Still, we stand only to gain from a careful examination of the history of readings of Paul's use of Isaiah. The fact that the subsequent tradition has made so much of Isaiah 53, despite the lack of explicit citations of the passage in Paul's letters, might suggest that there is a metaleptic suppression of Isaiah 53 in Paul that has worked effectively as a trope to highlight the uncited material.[37] In *Echoes*, I described the situation as follows:

> The letter to the Romans is salted with numerous quotations of and allusions to Isaiah 40-55, including several passages that seem to echo the Suffering Servant motif of Isaiah 53 (e.g., Romans 4.24-25, 5.15-19, 10.16, 15.21). Why, then, does Paul not draw this prophecy into the open and use the servant figure as an explicit basis for his interpretation of Israel, or of the church, or of Jesus? Paul's motive for this evasion or reticence, whichever it is, remains forever lost to us, but the effect of his rhetorical strategy can be readily described. He hints and whispers all around Isaiah 53 but never mentions the prophetic typology that would supremely integrate his interpretation of Christ and Israel. The result is a compelling example of metalepsis: Paul's transumptive silence cries out for the reader to complete the trope.[38]

Perhaps that is exactly what the history of interpretation in the Church has done.

Satisfaction
Does the proposed intertextual reading illuminate the surrounding discourse and make some larger sense of Paul's argument as a whole? This final criterion is elusive but important to the task of critical interpretation in the community. It is related to the criterion of thematic coherence (see above), but it differs in the following way: whereas the criterion of thematic coherence asks whether the content of an individual precursor text is materially related to the sense of Paul's argument at the place where the putative echo occurs (see examples above), the criterion of satisfaction asks more broadly whether the resultant reading of Paul's discussion is clarified and enhanced by an awareness of the proposed intertexts. This criterion calls for an integrative act of discernment about the meaning of the epistle as a whole, or at least the meaning of the local context within the epistle, in light of the proposed intertextual links. A proposed intertextual reading fulfills the test of satisfaction when we find ourselves saying, 'Oh, so *that* is what Paul means here in passage X; and furthermore, if that's right, then we can begin to understand what he means in passage Y and why he uses *these* certain words in that place.' For example, if Isaiah 40—55 really does play the role in Romans that

I have been proposing here, then our understanding of Romans 1.16–17, the keynote of the letter, will be illuminated by reading it in counterpoint with Isaiah 51.4–5 (my translation):

> Hear me, hear, my people,
> And kings, give ear to me.
> For the Law will go forth from me,
> And my judgement will go forth as a light to the Gentiles [ἐθνῶν],
> My righteousness [ἡ δικαιοσύνη μου] draws near quickly,
> And my salvation [τὸ σωτήριόν μου] will go forth as a light,
> And in my arm [cf. δύναμις in Romans 1.16] will Gentiles [ἔθνη] hope.

Or again, Isaiah 52.10:

> And the Lord will reveal [ἀποκαλύψει] his holy arm before all the Gentiles [ἐθνῶν],
> And all the corners of the earth will see the salvation [σωτηρίαν] that is with God.

I leave it to the reader to decide whether some such account of the good news is the message (εὐαγγέλιον in Romans 1.16, echoing Isaiah 52.7; ἀκοή in Romans 10.16, quoting Isaiah 53.1) that Paul believed himself commissioned to proclaim.

IV. Paul's Reading of Isaiah's Story: The Explicit Quotations

A full study of Paul's reading of Isaiah should begin with an inductive examination of all the passages in the letters where Paul quotes Isaiah explicitly. Such an examination should ask what motifs Paul spotlights in the text of Isaiah and how these motifs are related to the argument of the letters in which the quotations appear. Further, an attempt should be made to see whether these motifs can be plotted as part of a coherent narrative structure. In a paper of this length, such an inductive survey is impossible, but I will nonetheless venture a synthetic statement of the findings that I believe would issue from such a survey.

Paul reads Isaiah as having narrated beforehand the events that have at last been set in motion in Paul's generation through the death and resurrection of Jesus. These events may be summarized in the following way:

1. Israel has fallen into hard-hearted disobedience; their iniquities have separated them from God. Their disloyalty to the covenant brings discredit to God's name among the nations. Despite God's long-suffering fidelity to the covenant, Israel is 'a disobedient and contrary people'.

Isaiah 59.7–8 = Romans 3.15–17
Isaiah 52.5 = Romans 2.24
Isaiah 65.2 = Romans 10.21

2. Even so, God has not abandoned Israel. He has preserved a remnant of those who remain faithful.

Isaiah 1.9 = Romans 9.29
Isaiah 10.22 = Romans 9.27

3. God has now acted to bring the promise of eschatological salvation into fulfilment in the present time. But he has done so in a way that calls for trust (in Christ), causing the majority of Israel to stumble. Those who trust him will not be put to shame.

Isaiah 49.8 = 2 Corinthians 6.2 (cf. Isaiah 43.18 : 2 Corinthians 5.17)
Isaiah 8.14 = Romans 9.32–3
Isaiah 28.16 = Romans 9.33, 10.11

4. This is the message that Paul, apostle to the Gentiles, has been called to announce to the nations. Contrary to all expectation, the Gentiles are receiving this good news gladly. The Gentile mission is bearing fruit.

Isaiah 52.7 = Romans 10.15 (cf. Isaiah 49.1 : Galatians 1.15)
Isaiah 11.10 = Romans 15.12
Isaiah 45.14 = 1 Corinthians 14.25
Isaiah 52.15 = Romans 15.21
Isaiah 54.1 = Galatians 4.27 (a revisionary interpretation of Isaiah 54.1, reading Sarah as mother of the 'children of promise' (= Gentile believers))[39]
Isaiah 65.1 = Romans 10.20

5. But not all believe, because the message is an affront to human wisdom. In the present time, both Israel and the Gentile world are full of people who consider themselves wise, though actually they are blind and foolish. God will bring judgement upon them. In a mysterious way, God's judgement on disobedient Israel has taken the form of closing their eyes and hardening their hearts.

Isaiah 53.1 = Romans 10.16
Isaiah 22.13 = 1 Corinthians 15.32
Isaiah 28.11 = 1 Corinthians 14.21
Isaiah 29.14 = 1Corinthians 1.19
Isaiah 29.16, 45.9 = Romans 9.20
Isaiah 29.10 = Romans 11.8 (cf. also Isaiah 6.9–10)
Isaiah 65.2 = Romans 10.21

6. Nonetheless, in the end God will redeem Israel, forgive their sin, and establish sovereignty over the whole world, so that every knee will bow and every tongue give praise to God. This divine eschatological triumph will include God's overcoming the power of death.

Isaiah 27.9 = Romans 11.27
Isaiah 59.20 = Romans 11.27
Isaiah 45.23 = Romans 14.11 (cf. Philippians 2.10–11)
Isaiah 25.8 = 1 Corinthians 15.54

7. God's mercy is finally overwhelming and incomprehensible.

Isaiah 40.13 = Romans 11.34, 1 Corinthians 2.16.
Isaiah 64.4? = 1 Corinthians 2.9

All of this Paul finds foretold in Isaiah. It should be noted that, with the possible (and contested) exception of the 'stone of stumbling' (Isaiah 8.14+28.16 = Romans 9.32–3), Paul does not resort to christological typology in his interpretation of Isaiah. The story that he reads in the Isaiah scroll is closely constrained by Isaiah's original plotline of Israel's exile and restoration, accompanied by God's radical eschatological renewal that embraces the whole Gentile world.

V. Conclusion: Theses for Disputation

The limited goals of this paper have been to set forth some criteria for identifying allusions and echoes of the Old Testament in Paul, to make some observations about the application of these criteria to some illustrative passages where Paul seems to be echoing Isaiah, and to sketch the story-line implied by Paul's explicit citations of this prophetic book. To carry the investigation to its conclusion, we would have to comb thoroughly through the letters seeking possible allusions to Isaiah and evaluating them one by one. That is far too large an undertaking for the present essay. I have not, for example, taken up the familiar debates about whether we should hear allusions to Isaiah 53 in Romans 4.24-5, Romans 5.15-19, 1 Corinthians 15.3, and Philippians 2.6-11. Readers who find my proposed criteria useful can take up the task of applying them to these texts. I offer, however, in conclusion, a number of summary remarks and provocations.

1. Paul reads in Isaiah the story of God's eschatological redemption of the world. His extensive allusions to Isaiah 40—55 suggest that Paul has pondered this text repeatedly and found in it a prefiguration of his own apostolic mission to announce God's good news to the Gentile world. Or, to put the same point the other way around, Paul's reading of Isaiah is shaped by his own experience of the Gentile mission. The claim that Paul does see there a coherent *story*, not merely a grab-bag of isolated oracles, is very important for understanding his interpetation of the texts which he cites and echoes.

2. Paul's primary interest in his actual *use* of Isaiah does not seem to be christological. Here, as elsewhere, his hermeneutic is ecclesiocentric, focusing on the manifestation and operation of God's grace in the Church, the eschatological people of God. This is related to the concrete purpose of Paul's letters: Romans, for example, is not a treatise on christology but a theological reflection on the outworking of God's mysterious purposes for Jews and Gentiles in the drama of salvation. Thus, christology remains at an implicit, presuppositional level in the argument. That is why we find in Romans only allusions and echoes of early christological readings of the Old Testament. Paul was not so much interested in proving that Jesus 'was' the Servant. Rather, Paul was seeking to show that Isaiah revealed the prophetic promise of God's redemption of the world, embracing Gentiles as well as Jews. Consequently, we must keep reminding ourselves that Paul might have alluded to Isaiah for purposes other than those that have propelled much modern scholarly investigation.

3. Where we find citations and allusions in Paul's letters, we must always ask what they are doing in the argument, how they serve Paul's rhetorical and theological agenda. That is, we should come back again and again to the question of how the proposed intertextual collocations shape our reading of the epistles. There is an inescapable hermeneutical circle here: if our hypotheses about intertextual links yield illuminating readings of the letters, this result will increase our confidence about the validity of the hypotheses.

4. Paul was formed deeply by his reading of scripture. One consequence of this is that he may from time to time echo texts unconsciously or in passing, without thinking through all the possible implications of the intertextual links created by his own discourse. Later readers may recognize Paul's echoes of Isaiah and legitimately develop some theological implications of the intertextual links that had not occurred to Paul himself. It is possible (though in my view not likely) that the christological reading of Isaiah 53 could fall into this category.

5. We should give Paul and his readers credit for being at least as sophisticated and nuanced in their reading of scripture as we are. Everything about Paul's use of Old Testament texts suggests that his 'implied reader' not only knows scripture but also appreciates allusive subtlety. Whether the reader accepts the compliment or not, the apostle still delights in intertextual play.

6. Finally, there is the matter of what sort of readers we must be to read Paul's texts rightly. He calls upon his readers to present their bodies as a living sacrifice and to be transformed by the renewing of their minds. That is not exactly a *criterion* for rightly identifying allusions; it is something more like a *prerequisite*. As I have argued at length in *Echoes*, Paul believes that the veil over scripture is lifted only for those who turn to the Lord and that the meaning of scripture becomes clear only as the Spirit works to embody the sense of the text in concretely transformed communities.[40] If that is right, Paul's allusive texts will not yield up their treasures to the merely curious (sobering word for us scholars): they will speak only to those actively engaged in carrying out the ministry of reconciliation by embodying the righteousness of God, as a light to the nations.

Notes

1 The total of 89 Old Testament quotations is taken from D. A. Koch, *Die Schrift als Zeuge des Evangeliums: Untersuchungen zur Verwendung und zum Verständnis der Schrift bei Paulus* (BHT 69), Tübingen: J. C. B. Mohr (Paul Siebeck), 1986, pp. 21–4. The tabulation of 31 quotations of Isaiah is my own, based on the list of 'Loci Citati vel Allegati' in Nestle–Aland, 27th edn, pp. 789–93. According to Koch's tally (p. 33), there are 28 citations of Isaiah in the authentic letters.

2 These themes are discussed in J. Ross Wagner, 'The Heralds of Isaiah and the Mission of Paul', in W. H. Bellinger, Jr. and W. R. Farmer (eds), *Jesus and the Suffering Servant: Isaiah 53 and Christian Origins*, Harrisburg, PA.:

Trinity Press International, 1998, pp. 193–222. See also Wagner, *Heralds of the Good News: Isaiah and Paul 'In Concert' in the Letter to the Romans* (NovT Supp 101, Leiden: Brill, 2002).

3 'In the writings of the theologians of the early Church, we found little evidence that the identification of Jesus with the Servant played any great part in the thinking of St Paul, St John, or the author of the Epistle to the Hebrews, and no *proof* that it was known to them at all': M. Hooker, *Jesus and the Servant: The Influence of the Servant Concept of Deutero-Isaiah in the New Testament*, London: SPCK, 1959, p. 127.

4 For explanation of my use of this term, see R. B. Hays, *Echoes of Scripture in the Letters of Paul*, New Haven: Yale University Press, 1989, pp. 84–7.

5 For purposes of comparison, see J. Marcus, *The Way of the Lord: Christological Exegesis in the Gospel of Mark*, Louisville: Westminster/John Knox, 1992; R. Watts, *Isaiah's New Exodus and Mark* (WUNT, 2.88); Tübingen: J. C. B. Mohr (Paul Siebeck), 1997.

6 For text-critical reasons, the majority of commentators regard Romans 16:25–7 as an interpolation, rather than as a part of the original text of Romans. For discussion and further references, see, e.g., J. D. G. Dunn, *Romans 9–16* (WBC 38B), Dallas: Word, 1988, pp. 912–13; J. A. Fitzmyer, *Romans* (AB 33), New York: Doubleday, 1993, pp. 753–6. Even if these verses are secondary, the relation that they describe between gospel, Scripture, and proclamation to the Gentiles is an apt summary of Paul's argument in Romans; thus, at the very least, these words represent a well-informed reading of Pauline theology by an early editor of the Pauline corpus. My own inclination is to regard Romans 16.25–7 as Paul's own original and rather elegant conclusion to the letter, not least because the passage provides, along with Romans 1.1–7, a satisfying *inclusio*.

7 I continue to believe (as I suggested in *Echoes of Scripture in the Letters of Paul*, p. 85) that the prepositional phrase περὶ τοῦ υἱοῦ αὐτοῦ is most naturally to be read as modifying γραφαῖς ἁγίαις, rather than εὐαγγέλιον θεοῦ, so that the the sentence should be read as follows: '. . . which he promised beforehand in holy writings concerning his Son, who came from the seed of David according to the flesh . . .' My present point does not depend on this construal of the sentence, though this reading is not unrelated to the problem of the role of Isaiah 53 in Paul's christology. It should also be recalled, as noted above, that the conclusion of Romans associates τὸ κήρυγμα Ἰησοῦ Χριστοῦ with the revelation of a hidden mystery that is now disclosed through 'prophetic Scriptures' (διὰ γραφῶν προφητικῶν) to all the Gentiles (Romans 16.25–6).

8 According to the count of Koch (*Schrift als Zeuge*, p. 88), there are 65 Old Testament quotations in Romans, 56 of them explicitly marked as such.

9 Not long ago, while on sabbatical in Jerusalem, I met an American doctoral student who informed me that her New Testament professor at an

American graduate school had told his class that there are actually no Old Testament quotations in Paul's letters. All the apparent quotations, he said, are actually better explained on the basis of Graeco-Roman parallels! This absurd claim demonstrates the lengths to which some scholars will go to sever Paul from his Jewish roots.

10 I explored some aspects of this problem in *Echoes of Scripture in the Letters of Paul*. For a brief discussion of the state of the question prior to my work, see *Echoes*, pp. 5–14.

11 That is by no means to say that his symbolic world is shaped *only* by Scripture. Many other factors are part of the mix: the social and political realities of his day, popular Graeco-Roman philosophical traditions, the distinctive experiences and traditions of the emergent Christian movement, and so forth.

12 Thomas M. Greene, *The Light in Troy: Imitation and Discovery in Renaissance Poetry*, New Haven: Yale University Press, 1982, p. 53.

13 Hooker, *Jesus and the Servant*, p. 62, italics in original. This quotation comes from her chapter on 'The Servant in the Synoptic Gospels' rather than from her discussion of Paul, but her aims are constant throughout. She is seeking definitive proof that the New Testament's language has come exclusively from a particular source.

14 For bringing this example to my attention and for much fascinating conversation about it I am indebted to Christopher B. Hays.

15 'And Thou sentest Thine hand from above and drewest [*eruisti*] my soul out of that profound darkness.' English translations here are taken from *The Confessions of Saint Augustine*, trans. E. B. Pusey, New York: Modern Library, 1949. I have not been able to determine what translation (if any) Eliot was using. 'Pluckest' is actually a very good – and far more vivid – translation of *eruisti*.

16 Hays, *Echoes*, pp. 29–33.

17 J. Hollander, *The Figure of Echo: A Mode of Allusion in Milton and After*, Berkeley: University of California Press, 1981.

18 Actually, even ἀρχαῖα is lacking in Isaiah 65.17, which refers only to τῶν προτέρων. On the other hand, the 'new heaven and new earth' of Isaiah 65.17 certainly suggests – even more clearly than Isaiah 43:18–19 – the Pauline idea of a 'new creation'.

19 For the most comprehensive study of this problem, see Christopher D. Stanley, *Paul and the Language of Scripture: Citation Technique in the Pauline Epistles and Contemporary Literature* (SNTSMS 69), Cambridge: Cambridge University Press, 1992.

20 Of course, it is equally possible that later Christian scribes copying the Greek Old Testament might have altered the text to conform to Paul's citations; such problems must be assessed on a case-by-case basis.

21 For an illustration of how I think such problems should be handled, see my

treatment of the possible echo of the Masoretic Text's image of God as Rock (Deuteronomy 32.4, 15, 18, 30, 31) in 1 Corinthians 10.4 (*Echoes*, p. 94).

22 In 1 Corinthians 8, context also plays a role: the fact that Paul is contrasting Christian confession to polytheistic idolatry helps to confirm the resonance of the Shema behind 1 Corinthians 8; this again shows how the criterion of thematic coherence (see p. 57) comes into play to complement other criteria.

23 Hays, *Echoes*, pp. 30, 152–3. See my further suggestion there (p. 153) that 2 Corinthians 4.6 also echoes Isaiah 9.2.

24 For a full discussion see R. H. Bell, *Provoked to Jealousy: The Origin and Purpose of the Jealousy Motif in Romans 9–11* (WUNT 2.63), Tübingen: J. C. B. Mohr (Paul Siebeck), 1994.

25 I noted this phenomenon in *Echoes* (p. 30), but did not develop its significance sufficiently.

26 This figure was devised by Diana Swancutt, Assistant Professor of New Testament at Yale Divinity School. I use this material here with her permission and with gratitude to her.

27 One of these, however, the quotation of Isaiah 49.18 in Romans 14.11, should probably be described as an echo rather than a quotation.

28 Wagner, 'Heralds', p. 194.

29 As Wagner notes, Paul has converted Isaiah's singular messenger to a plural (τῶν εὐαγγελιζομένων), without warrant in any extant Greek or Hebrew text of Isaiah. This shows that Paul interpreted the passage not christologically but as a reference to the (plural) Christian preachers of the gospel.

30 Here again we note that Paul's lone citation of a passage from Isaiah 53 focuses not on the mysterious figure of the Servant but on the activity of those who have proclaimed the message about him – a message met by the hearers with considerable scepticism.

31 Hooker, *Jesus and the Servant*, pp. xi–xii. She describes this as one of the two main points that emerge from her study of the problem.

32 For discussion, see G. J. Brooke, *Exegesis at Qumran: 4Q Florilegium in its Jewish Context* (JSOTSup 29), Sheffield: JSOT, 1985, pp. 197–205; D. Juel, *Messianic Exegesis: Christological Interpretation of the Old Testament in Early Christianity*, Philadelphia: Fortress, 1988, pp. 69–77; Hays, *Echoes*, p. 85.

33 For discussion of this example, see Hays, *Echoes*, pp. 77–82. In a response to my work, Craig A. Evans has also pointed out that Targum Neofiti on Deuteronomy 30.12–13 fills in even more possible background for Paul's interpretation of Deuteronomy 30. See Craig A. Evans, 'Listening for Echoes of Interpreted Scripture', in C. A. Evans and J. A. Sanders (eds), *Paul and the Scriptures of Israel* (JSNTSup 83), Sheffield: JSOT, 1993, pp. 47–51.

34 A recent collection of essays, B. Janowski and P. Stuhlmacher (eds), *Der leidende Gottesknecht: Jesaja 53 und seine Wirkungsgeschichte* (Forschungen zum

Alten Testament 14), Tübingen: J. C. B. Mohr (Paul Siebeck), 1996, is a step in the right direction, but by focusing only on Isaiah 53 it runs the risk of drawing the circle of attention too narrowly and thus prejudging the questions I am seeking to raise here.

35 Wagner prefers to speak of a 'missiological hermeneutic'.
36 Cf. Hollander, *Figure of Echo*, pp. 65–6.
37 In brief, 'metalepsis' is a rhetorical figure that creates a correspondence between two texts such that text B should be understood in light of a broad interplay with the precursor text A, encompassing aspects of A beyond those explicitly cited. See Hays, *Echoes*, pp. 18–21. For an informative discussion tracing the history of this terminology back at least to Quintilian, see Hollander, *Figure of Echo*, pp. 133–49.
38 Hays, *Echoes*, p. 63.
39 See Hays, *Echoes*, pp. 105–21.
40 Hays, *Echoes*, pp. 122–53.

6

Paul, Scripture and Ethics

Christopher Tuckett

The general question I want to address in this article is a relatively narrow one: in considering the use made by New Testament writers of Old Testament texts, whether in explicit citations or in more implicit echoes or allusions, how far should one take account of the wider context within the Old Testament from which the citation or allusion is taken? Such a question has been answered in positive terms by a number of scholars in recent years in relation to a wide range of New Testament texts.[1]

The question can be taken at a number of different levels. We can consider the authors of the New Testament texts: how far did one author, in referring to an Old Testament text, have in mind the broader context from which the text has come? We can ask about the first 'readers' of the text:[2] how far would/did the initial readers recognize and take account of the broader context? We can bracket off the historical question and simply ask whether we as readers might/can/should take account of the broader context of a quotation or allusion in order to enrich our understanding of the New Testament text. No doubt too there are a number of other hermeneutical possibilities, each with its own legitimacy within its own frame of reference.

In order to keep the discussion within manageable limits, the focus here will be primarily on one of these hermeneutical possibilities. In particular, I shall be adopting a broadly historical–critical approach in that I shall be considering how New Testament texts might have functioned in their original historical contexts. Further, within such an approach I will be concerned here primarily with the first *recipients* of the text: how

---

An earlier version of this chapter was delivered as a Main Paper at the 1999 Pretoria meeting of Studiorum Novi Testamenti Societas. I am grateful to Professors Christopher Rowland, Martin de Boer and Dr David Horrell, who kindly read an earlier draft of this essay and made helpful suggestions for improvement.

far might first-century readers/hearers of the New Testament texts have recognized and taken account of the broader contexts of Old Testament citations and allusions in the texts they read or heard? The question of how much first-century authors intended such contexts to be heard is of course also relevant; but the focus on the reader means that the question is not so much what an author may have had in mind, but how much of the broader context an author expected to be picked up by his readers/hearers and recognized as significant in interpreting a citation or allusion. The focus here will thus be primarily on New Testament texts as forms of communication between author and reader, and communication is primarily a two-way process involving both author and reader.

The question posed initially is in one way a relatively narrow one (it does not for example ask about the importance of the Old Testament generally for New Testament writers), yet it is clearly too wide-ranging to be treated with any adequacy in a single article. For example, to talk of 'the' Old Testament and 'the' New Testament in this context runs the real danger of generalizing too quickly. As we have all learnt as standard critical orthodoxy today, the New Testament is not a monolithic unity; equally, the Old Testament citations and allusions in the New Testament do not form a monolithic unity. Thus what applies to one writer may not apply to another. Further, the same writer may have adopted different strategies at different points.

In this article the focus will be on Paul alone, and clearly all the caveats just mentioned apply here. Very similar considerations also apply in relation to the recipients of Paul's letters. For example, it is well known that the Paul of Romans and Galatians is rather different from the Paul of 1 Thessalonians in the extent to which he cites scripture. Equally, the various recipients of Paul's letters may have been attuned in different ways to hear possible 'echoes' of broader contexts. Just as the Corinthian and Thessalonian Christian communities may have been different socially,[3] so too may have been their capacity to 'hear' unstated allusions to scripture in Paul's writings (and indeed Paul himself may have been aware of this).

We must also be alive to the fact that different Old Testament quotations or allusions may function in different ways. For example, reference to named individual Old Testament figures is clearly intended to evoke broader contexts and associated ideas. Thus the phrase 'the blood of Abel' in Luke 11.51 clearly evokes, and is intended to evoke, the whole story of the murder of Abel in Genesis 4, and unless this is picked up by the readers/hearers, any communication is lost completely. So too references to figures like Moses, David or Abraham would be meaningless without recourse to the stories and traditions associated with these figures in the Old Testament.

The same probably applies to key parts of Israel's history. With any society, the founding events that established the identity of that society will always have a key role in subsequent history.[4] Thus in the case of the nation of Israel, the events associated with the Exodus, including the giving of the Law at Sinai as well as the events of the wilderness wanderings as recounted in the Pentateuch, would be easily recalled and evoked in different contexts. So, for example, the failings of the Israelites at the time of the Exodus in the wilderness period could be, and were, used in various re-tellings of the story to encourage repentance and a renewal of commitment by later Jews (cf. Psalms 78, 106; Nehemiah 9; also the song of Moses in Deuteronomy 32). Paul's evoking of the same events in a similar way in 1 Corinthians 10.1–13 lies in the same tradition.[5]

More debatable perhaps is the use of prophetic and other texts not so clearly related to Israel's founding history and where no proper names are mentioned such as to make the locating of the citation/allusion in its original context inevitable. Here it is not so easy to find close parallels to the alleged phenomenon in non-Christian texts.[6] For example, the Qumran texts for the most part seem to have had a blithe disregard for any concern with the 'original' context when interpreting Old Testament prophetic texts: all the concern is with how the wording of the text relates to the new context to which the Qumran writer has chosen to apply the prophecy.[7] Nor is it easy to find parallels in Philo or Josephus.

In seeking to answer the question posed at the start of this paper, what criteria might one apply? The question is probably more easily posed than answered.[8] So too it is in one way far easier to stake a claim that the broader contexts of Old Testament quotations are in mind than to try to claim they are not. Certainly one can always develop theories which claim to show how the broader context of a citation or allusion has affected, and is intended to affect, what is said in a New Testament text. Sceptics can always then be chided for being blind or deaf and not having 'eyes to see or ears to hear'.[9] But how can we be sure that such theories have anything at all to do with how the New Testament texts were written, or heard, in the first century? How do we know that it is not simply our modern reading which hears and identifies the echoes of the wider context?

The main argument of this essay will be to try to argue the negative case, to claim that it is unlikely that much wider contexts were intended to be evoked afresh by authors to readers. Yet clear evidence for this is, by the very nature of the case, difficult to obtain. There are, though, two instances in the New Testament where adjacent Old Testament verses are cited consecutively, but apparently as separate quotations and with no awareness that the two verses were originally consecutive (cf. Luke 4.10–11, citing Psalm 91.11, 12, and Hebrews 2.13, citing Isaiah 8.17, 18).[10] So too Paul sometimes uses texts from originally closely related contexts in very different ways and in widely different contexts, suggesting that the original context of the quotation may not have been important for him.[11] Such examples are of course only isolated ones. Nevertheless, a consideration of some general and down-to-earth factors may be relevant here in suggesting the implausibility of positing more than a relatively limited awareness of broader literary contexts by the audience of New Testament texts.

First, we must remember that standards of literacy in the ancient world were not very high generally. It has been estimated that the number of people who were literate cannot have been much more than 20 per cent of the population as a whole and may have been considerably less.[12] Further, it is now widely accepted that early Christian groups were not from the lowest classes of society, but equally were not predominantly from the highest strata either.[13] It is thus unlikely that Christian communities were significantly more literate than the wider population in Hellenistic cities or elsewhere.[14]

All this means that in, say, Pauline communities, virtually all 'literature', be it Paul's own letters or Jewish scripture, would have been available to most members of the community in *oral* form: they would have *heard* it, rather than read it.[15] Any detailed awareness of a wider context of a quotation or allusion would have had to be based on at best recollection from memory, and this must make such a theory a little uncertain.

Second, we must remember that Jewish scriptures in Paul's day were presumably available only in scroll form, and probably in a number of different scrolls.[16] Locating allusions and citations in an original text in scroll form must have been a cumbersome and awkward procedure. Moreover, scrolls were expensive to produce and copies of Jewish scripture in scrolls were presumably only available to relatively few people (most, presumably, Jews).[17] This makes it further unlikely that first-century hearers (or the few readers around) would have encountered much of Jewish scripture in its 'original' literary context. Thus when most of Paul's hearers/readers encountered a citation or allusion by Paul from the Old Testament, the primary context will have been the literary context of Paul's letter and *his* citation.[18]

The nature of scrolls also makes it difficult to conceive that any very broad 'broader context' of an Old Testament verse was in the mind of any reader or hearer. An awareness of the broader context consisting of (what was later regarded as) a few 'verses' might be conceivable. (For example, a verse from Isaiah 53 *might* evoke the whole of the description of the 'servant' figure of that chapter.) But theories involving whole books are harder to conceive simply in physical terms: how could one reader easily hold in view (literally!) a passage from Deutero-Isaiah with the passage in Isaiah 9 about the ideal king?[19]

There is too the question whether the first readers of the New Testament texts were themselves Jews. If they were in fact Gentiles, how much access would they have had to copies of Jewish scripture?[20] No doubt some Gentile converts to Christianity may have had some contact with Jewish groups prior to their conversion.[21] But Gentiles will inevitably only have had limited access, and presumably also limited exposure, to Jewish scripture. Detailed knowledge of all of scripture and its contexts would thus presumably be the exception rather than the norm for Paul's audiences.

We can of course seek to find possible parallels to Christian communities in other Jewish groups using scripture,[22] and the obvious parallel phenomenon so often adduced is that of the Qumran literature. It is however not at all certain how close the two groups of literature really are. How far is there any *generic* similarity between Qumran texts and early Christian literature? (The closest parallel might be between Paul's letters and 4QMMT, but even here the similarities are not great.) Qumran does not contain anything looking remotely like a life of the Teacher of Righteousness or (with the exception of 4QMMT) letters directly addressing a group in another location. First-century Christianity did not produce a rule book for the conduct of its members (possibly excepting the *Didache*), nor did it (as far as we know) write out biblical texts or produce commentaries on such texts. Socially the two groups were dissimilar (Qumran lived in the desert, Christian groups in towns and cities), nor did Christian groups appear to have had the same degree of literary sophistication that is evident in much of the Qumran literature. In all it is doubtful how useful the comparison between the Qumran texts and the Pauline letters in their use of scripture really is.[23]

As stated earlier, blanket claims covering the use of the Old Testament in the whole New Testament, or even in one writer as a whole, are not easily sustainable. All one can do within the confines of a single article is to test a relatively small sample. Thus the focus here will be on some parts of Paul's argument in 1 Corinthians 1—5. Of course, this may be an atypical passage: Paul's use of scripture in 1 Corinthians 1—5 may be unlike the rest of Paul, or even other parts of 1 Corinthians. Nevertheless, it is a part of the Pauline corpus where Paul does refer to scripture and hence must be taken into account as part of the total picture of Paul's use of the Old Testament; moreover, it is a passage where some have claimed recently that Paul's debt to scripture goes deeper than a surface reading might suggest. It may therefore serve as a useful test passage.

If our concern is primarily with *readers*, how Paul's letters might have been read or heard by their initial recipients, then we must first ask about the Corinthians and their capacity to hear any possible echoes of scripture. Such a question is of course unanswerable with any certainty. We have nothing directly from the Corinthian Christians. Nevertheless, Paul's letters, together with other evidence, may help a little.[24] 1 Corinthians itself suggests that the Corinthians were not ignorant about Old Testament scripture (or at least Paul apparently thought they were not ignorant). Paul can, and does, remind them in 1 Corinthians 15.3 of a pre-Pauline formula about the death and resurrection of Jesus, a formula which clearly has a lot of interpretation built into it, viz. that 'Christ' died 'according to the scriptures' and that he was raised on the third day 'according to the scriptures'. Paul's language suggests that this is common ground to himself and the Corinthians: hence the Corinthians must have accepted the claim about κατὰ τὰς γραφάς. Of course we do not know how much substance they put into that general claim though it may be reasonable to assume that they thought such a claim could be substantiated. Similarly, in what may well be another pre-Pauline fragment (see p. 80), Paul's statement in 1 Corinthians 5.7 ('Christ our Passover is sacrificed for us') presupposes some familiarity with the feast of Passover, its symbolism and its ritual. In 1 Corinthians 10.1–13, Paul appeals to the example of the wilderness wanderings and evidently presupposes a certain amount of knowledge on the part of the Corinthians (the passage would be all but incomprehensible for any who had never heard the Exodus stories at all.)[25] In the middle of that section too, Paul makes the famous equation between the 'rock' of the wilderness wanderings and the person of Christ (v. 4), an equation that many have argued needs a middle stage, equating the rock with the 'person' of Wisdom, in order to be comprehensible.[26] Again it is notable that Paul does not stop to explain, let alone argue, his point here. He seems to assume that he can take it as read. Thus it would seem that the Corinthians may have had some knowledge of scripture already and indeed, in the last case, of Jewish traditions of interpreting scripture.[27] On the other hand, we may note Paul's passing remark in 12.2 that the Corinthians were Gentiles prior to their becoming Christians.[28]

At first sight these two pieces of data – the Corinthians having some knowledge of scripture and the Corinthians being Gentiles – might seem not easy to reconcile. If, though, we take the evidence of Acts into account, we may gain a reasonably plausible picture.[29] According to Acts 18, Paul goes first to the Jewish synagogue in Corinth before being driven out.[30] He then settles in the house next door belonging to a certain Titius Justus, who is said to be a person who 'worshipped God' (Acts 18.7). The synagogue official Crispus also became a Christian believer (v. 8). The general picture might then fit the evidence of 1 Corinthians itself reasonably well if we postulate the Corinthian community as made up largely of people who had been on the 'fringe' of Judaism, perhaps as 'God-fearers' (if such existed).[31] Thus it may not be unreasonable to postulate a certain amount of knowledge of Old Testament scripture on the part of the Corinthians. I turn then to a consideration of two possible examples of Paul's use of scripture in 1 Corinthians.

1 Corinthians 5.13
Paul's language in 1 Corinthians 5.13 ('Drive out the wicked person from among you') has been the subject of some debate in recent studies. The words are not prefaced by any introductory formula by Paul; yet the language used is very close to a number of verses in Deuteronomy[32] and indeed the Nestle–Aland text prints the words in italics, indicating the editors' view that this is some kind of 'quotation'. The lack of an introductory formula has led a number of scholars to ignore the verse in their studies of Paul's Old Testament quotations.[33] Others, however, notably Rosner and Hays, have argued more recently that the words should be seen as a quasi-quotation, indicating Paul's deep debt to the Old Testament in his ethical teaching.[34] The subject of the chapter is the question of a Corinthian man apparently having sexual relations with 'his father's wife' (v. 1), a practice explicitly forbidden in Deuteronomy 23.1 (Septuagint (LXX) 22.30). Further, one of the occurrences of the execution/exclusion formula in Deuteronomy comes in the close context of this verse, viz. in Deuteronomy 22.22.[35] Thus, it is argued, Paul's

instructions here are strongly influenced by the Deuteronomic legislation, and the allusion in v. 13 evokes the wider context from which it comes.

How much, though, would the Corinthians have heard or read from Paul's language here? We have already noted the lack of an introductory formula to the words of v. 13: hence it is not at all certain that, as Gentile readers with *some* – but not necessarily unlimited – knowledge of Jewish scripture, they would have recognized the words as scriptural at all.[36] Further, the words in question come at the very end of Paul's discussion of the issue. There has been no explicit reference to the law in Deuteronomy proscribing sexual relations with one's father's (or anyone else's) wife earlier in Paul's discussion. Would, then, Paul's readers have realized that his ethical decisions were based – in whole, in part, or even at all – on the Deuteronomic law before reaching v. 13? At the very least one would expect some allusion earlier in the discussion if any 'echo' in v. 13 was to have been 'heard' by the Corinthians.

Rosner has, however, argued that such allusions might be present. He suggests that the Deuteronomic legislation about expulsion is governed by three factors: the idea of covenant obligations, an idea of corporate responsibility, and also an idea of holiness; moreover, he claims that the same ideas recur in Paul.[37] Yet it is hard to see much of this in the rest of 1 Corinthians 5. Certainly the idea of specifically *covenant* obligation is not clear in Paul's language. Paul starts the chapter by noting that the behaviour of the Corinthian man would not even be tolerated 'among the Gentiles'. The implication seems to be that the ethic Paul is promoting, viz. that living with one's father's wife is morally unacceptable, is one which would command universal assent, i.e. from Gentiles as well as Jews. There is then no appeal here to specifically Jewish ideas of *covenant* obligation; rather, the appeal is to what is claimed to be the universal moral rejection of such behaviour.

Rosner also seeks to reinforce the covenantal and/or Deuteronomic basis for Paul's argument by referring to the vice list in 1 Corinthians 5.11–12: he claims that Paul's list of vices can be seen to correspond to the list of offences in Deuteronomy for which the exclusion/banning order is ordained.[38] However, the alleged correspondences are at times rather weak. For example, the parallels drawn between the person who gives malicious false testimony (Deuteronomy 19.18–19) and Paul's 'reviler' (λοίδορος), or between the rebellious son who is a profligate and a drunkard (Deuteronomy 21.20–1) and Paul's 'drunkard' (μέθυσος), or between a kidnapper (Deuteronomy 24.7) and Paul's 'robber' (ἅρπαξ), are very general. In any case, as Rosner admits, sexual immorality and idolatry (Deuteronomy 17.3, 7; Deuteronomy 22) are often linked both in Paul (cf. Romans 1.19–27; 1 Corinthians 6.9–10; Galatians 5.19–21) and by others, so that we do not necessarily need the Deuteronomic exclusion formulae to explain their being linked here. In view of the very general nature of some of the parallels, it seems highly unlikely that any Gentile readers/hearers of Paul would have picked up the alleged set of parallels, even if they may have been in Paul's mind.

It is also not easy to see any idea of corporate responsibility reflected in Paul's language. It has been argued that Paul's demand in v. 2, that the Corinthians should not have been 'puffed up' but should rather have 'mourned', is an indication of this, implying a demand for repentance; and parallels have been sought in e.g. the figure of Ezra mourning for the sins of the people (cf. Ezra 10.6; 1 Esdras 8.72, 9.2).[39] However, 'mourning' takes place in a wide range of contexts and it is difficult to press the meaning of the word on its own, without any other contextual indications, into a meaning of repenting, let alone repenting for *corporate* sins.

Nor does the example of Ezra really provide a clear parallel to what is alleged here. In Ezra 10.6, Ezra does indeed 'mourn', but there seems little suggestion that Ezra himself is accepting responsibility for the sins of others: when Ezra then addresses the people, it is all in the second person, not the first person (v. 10: '*you* have trespassed and married foreign women'; v. 11: 'separate *yourselves*'; etc.). There is clearly a corporate idea here, as there is in other parts of the Old Testament.[40] But it is very doubtful whether any idea of corporate *responsibility* or *guilt* is implied in the references to 'mourning' alone.

In fact Paul here clearly distinguishes the incestuous man and the Corinthians, both with respect to the sin committed and the punishment. He is guilty of incest (v. 1), they are guilty of pride and arrogance (v. 2); he is to be handed over to Satan (v. 5),[41] they are not. Hence it is hard to see any idea here of corporate *guilt* being imputed to the rest of the Corinthian community by Paul. They are indeed not without blame in Paul's view: but that is because of their *reaction* to the man's behaviour, not because they are deemed to be guilty of the same incestuous actions themselves. It is thus very doubtful whether there is any idea here of corporate responsibility.

That there is some idea of holiness implied here is undeniable.[42] But whether this is connected to the Deuteronomic legislation explicitly seems very unclear. Once again we may doubt how far any reader of Paul could have related Paul's instructions in 1 Corinthians 5.1–12 with Deuteronomy via such a general theme before the allusion/quotation in v. 13.

In fact, if Old Testament legislation does lie behind Paul's instructions here, Paul's language in v. 3 and his use of the first-person singular ('*I* have decided' how to deal with the situation) seems extremely odd. If the basis for the decision is that the Old Testament law of Deuteronomy is held to be still valid for the situation of the Corinthian Christian community, then one would surely expect a clear reference to this here. The decision would not be a human decision but that of God himself as the legislator of Deuteronomy. But v. 3 says that the decision is being made by Paul himself.

Paul himself does seek to explain his decision in the verses which follow. Perhaps, in seeking to discover the basis of Paul's own ethic, as well as how Paul's ethic might have been heard or read by others, we would do well to find the primary evidence in what Paul himself actually says: presumably Paul's first readers could at least be forgiven for thinking that the basis for Paul's ethical teaching is what Paul actually says is the basis for his teaching![43]

Paul's argument in 1 Corinthians 5.1–12 has nothing to do with the Deuteronomic legislation at all. It is in fact something of a 'hotch-potch' of different 'arguments' or claims. There is the general 'christological' appeal to the fact that the Corinthian community will be gathered together with Paul present 'in spirit' and will make their decision in the name, and by the power, of the Lord Jesus.[44] He then appeals to a general proverb about the contamination engendered by leaven (v. 6), a proverb which Paul uses elsewhere (Galatians 5.9) and for which there are clear non-Jewish parallels as well.[45] This proverb is then applied and developed in slightly confusing ways. In one development, what is bad is seen as *old* leaven which must presumably be replaced by new, fresh leaven (v. 7a, 8aβ); but this is then developed into a contrast between leaven itself, which is taken as bad, and a situation of no leaven (vv. 7b, 8bβ). And this idea of 'unleaven' in turn leads to the idea of Passover and the parallel/typology drawn between the death of Jesus and the sacrifice of the Passover lamb (vv. 7b, 8a). There is almost certainly a tradition being used here.[46] Possibly too the tradition had already 'ethicized' the imagery, associating 'leaven' with malice (κακία) and wickedness (πονηρία), and 'no leaven' with sincerity (εἰλικρινεία) and truth (ἀληθεία). None of these four terms correlates very closely with the situation Paul is addressing in 1 Corinthians 5: the Corinthians and the Corinthian man are not necessarily guilty of 'malice', and 'wickedness' is very general;[47] and the 'virtues' of 'sincerity' and 'truth' are not the obvious antitheses of the Corinthian attitude of being 'puffed up'. Hence it seems most likely that Paul is taking up a tradition which compared Jesus' death with the Passover sacrifice and which had already developed this symbolism in an ethical direction via the leaven/unleaven motif.

All this suggests that the primary basis for Paul's argument here is the *christological* claim about the nature and significance of Jesus' death seen as a Passover sacrifice, with general ethical implications already drawn from this by an earlier tradition. And all this is then applied to the situation in Corinth by reference to a moral judgement which Paul believes – and states – can be assumed as universally accepted (v. 1). Insofar then as the community is to rid itself of the incestuous man, the idea is probably more related to the Passover ritual of getting rid of 'leaven' (here taken as symbolic of evil and wickedness) than it is in terms of Deuteronomic legislation of execution or expulsion.

All this does, then, presuppose some knowledge of the Old Testament and of Jewish customs on the part of the readers/hearers. But it is knowledge of the Passover, and the rituals associated with that feast, not of Deuteronomic legislation and the sanctions laid down there. Such knowledge would not however be unprecedented and it seems not unreasonable to think of Gentiles on the fringe of Judaism having some awareness and knowledge of the Passover rituals as practised by Jews, perhaps too with some awareness of an interpretation of leaven/unleaven in ethical terms.[48] But in any case it is here a heavily Christianized Passover symbolism, referring to Jesus and his death, that is presupposed by Paul. Thus, for Paul, Christology (at least in general terms) is the overriding consideration in his ethical teaching here. The Old Testament legislation of Deuteronomy does *not* seem to be an important factor in Paul's argument. Such legislation *may* have been in the background of Paul's thinking. But it is hard to see that this would have been picked up in any way by Paul's audience on the basis of what Paul actually says in vv. 1–12 at least. V. 13 may simply represent at most a use of biblical terminology or phraseology with no further overtones detectable, at least to readers. It thus seems very improbable that Paul's language here would have led his readers to any wider context of Deuteronomy. Nor is there any indication that Paul would have wished to lead them in that direction. They had surely been led – by Paul! – down other avenues of biblical imagery already. Any 'echo' engendered by Paul's language in v. 13 would appear to be strictly limited.

1 Corinthians 1.31

The other Old Testament quotation to be examined here is Paul's quotation in 1 Corinthians 1.31. Unlike 1 Corinthians 5.13 this is explicitly signalled by Paul as an Old Testament quotation with the introductory formula καθὼς γέγραπται. There is however a slight uncertainty about what this is actually a quotation of: most assume that it is a quotation (albeit involving some substantial abbreviation) of Jeremiah 9.23–4 (Masoretic Text; 9.22–3 LXX). However, the same saying appears in the LXX version of the song of Hannah in 1 Kingdoms 2.10; and a strong case has recently been made for the view that it is the latter that is in mind rather than Jeremiah.[49] As will be seen, I am in agreement with this view, but for rather different reasons, and I draw rather different conclusions. In one sense, the issue may be immaterial since Jeremiah 9.23–4 and 1 Kingdoms 2.10 LXX are all but identical.[50] My primary concern is how far, if at all, the wider context of the quotation in the Old Testament is in view.

In this instance a strong case can be made for the slightly wider context of the words being in Paul's mind here. Jeremiah 9.23–4 and 1 Kingdoms 2.10 LXX have the words which Paul 'quotes' as part of a longer oracle:

> Let not the wise man boast in his wisdom, let not the mighty man boast in his might, let not the rich man boast in his riches, but let him who boasts boast in this, that he understands and knows me, that I am the Lord, who practises kindness, justice and righteousness in the earth. (Jeremiah 9.23–4 MT)

Paul's words in 1 Corinthians 1.31 represent an abbreviated version of the final positive clause of this oracle.[51] Yet just a few verses earlier, Paul seems to have the negative parts of the same oracle in mind when he tells the Corinthians that 'not many of you were wise by human standards, not many were powerful, not many were of noble birth' (1.26). Many have seen Paul's triad here of 'wise–powerful–noble birth' as engendered by the triad from the oracle in Jeremiah, 'wise–mighty–wealthy', thus providing clear evidence that Paul did have a wider Old Testament context in mind than just the part he has actually quoted in v. 31.[52]

One difference between Paul and the Old Testament oracle may be noted here. The Old Testament oracle tells those who (think they) *are* wise and powerful not to boast in their own wisdom and power; and yet Paul (on the usual reading of 1 Corinthians 1.26) seems to presuppose that his Corinthian addressees were *not* wise or powerful.[53] How then could the fuller oracle of Jeremiah 9/1 Kingdoms 2 be relevant to them?

This may be related to another difference between Paul and the Old Testament: the parallelism between 1 Corinthians 1.26–31 and the oracle in Jeremiah 9 does not involve identity in the wording of the triads. Above all, Paul does not refer to the 'rich' here, but to those of 'noble birth'.[54] It may be that Paul is aware of the fact that, at one level, the community is reasonably well-off financially and not destitute: certainly Paul can presume later that they have enough money to be able to set aside some surplus for his collection (cf. 1 Corinthians 16.1; 2 Corinthians 8). But, although fairly well-to-do materially, they may not have been of very high status socially.[55] Hence Paul may have changed the third term of the triad to find a point of (negative) agreement: they can indeed agree that very few of them were of noble birth, whereas they perhaps would not agree that they were materially poor and not 'rich'.[56] Thus 1 Corinthians 1.26 seems to be formulated as an indicative statement in negative terms about the Corinthians' situation and status with which they will agree.

But if the oracle of Jeremiah 9/1 Kingdoms 2 is in the background throughout 1 Corinthians 1.26–31, how much of the broader context of the text actually cited in v. 31 may have been in Paul's mind *and* could have been picked up by the Corinthians themselves? Hays suggests that the whole section in Jeremiah 8.3—9.26 may be in mind: 'a repeated theme of this unit is that the people who claim to be wise will soon incur God's judgement (e.g. Jeremiah 8.9 'The wise shall be put to shame, they shall be dismayed and taken; since they have rejected the word of the Lord, what wisdom is there in them?')'.[57] It is however hard to envisage any Corinthian readers/hearers making such a connection. The alleged unit in Jeremiah 8—9 is very long and it is some 35 verses back to the alleged key verse of 8.9. In any case the section is not very clearly about false *wisdom* (the word occurs only rarely in the section). Given all the general problems noted earlier about the nature of the accessibility of scriptural texts, it seems unlikely that any Corinthian reader of Paul's argument would have gone so far afield in bringing in the wider context in this way.

As in 1 Corinthians 5, Paul's explicit citation with the introductory formula does not occur until the very end of the section. If then it is Paul who brings in the wider context, it is hard to see how the Corinthians would have known that there was an Old Testament text, *and* its associated context, to pick up until the clear marker given by Paul in v. 31.[58]

As already noted, the majority of Paul's addressees would presumably have heard, rather than read, his words. Hence it would have been very hard, if not impossible, to retrace steps backwards to an earlier part of an oral text and recognize echoes in words that had previously been spoken. Further, Paul's possible allusion to the oracle in 1 Corinthians 1.26 changes at least one of the three terms of the triad from 'rich' to 'noble birth' (see above). If this were all new to the Corinthians, they would have had to recognize an allusion that had altered the text significantly at one point. On the other hand, the tie-up between Paul's language in v. 26 and the oracle in Jeremiah/1 Kingdoms is extremely striking and seems scarcely accidental. All this suggests that if the 'echoes' of the fuller oracle were heard by the Corinthians – and the close tie-up between v. 26 and v. 31 suggests that they were – *the Corinthians had the oracle already in mind.*[59]

But how might the oracle have been used? It is widely agreed that in 1 Corinthians 1—4, Paul is addressing a problem of an overvaluing of σοφία on the part of the Corinthians. However, Paul's language may suggest a varying level of 'wisdom' on the part of the Corinthians. For example, 1 Corinthians 4.8 is widely held to be Paul's sarcastic reflection of Corinthian claims for themselves: they are 'filled', they are 'rich', they have become 'kings' and are 'reigning' in some sense. So too, the language of 4.10 probably echoes (with heavy irony on Paul's part) the Corinthian claims: they are 'wise' (φρόνιμοι), 'strong' (ἰσχυροί) and 'held in honour' (ἔνδοξοι), language very similar to 1.26. But in 1.26, Paul seems to assume that the Corinthians will accept that they were *not* σοφοί, δυνατοί, εὐγενεῖς. How are these passages to be reconciled?

One possibility is that the two claims refer to different times. The claims reflected in 4.8, 10 presumably refer to the present state of the Corinthians: they are now wise, rich, reigning etc. Paul's appeal in 1.26 is rather to their circumstances when they were 'called' (to be Christians):[60] then they were (mostly) not wise by human standards, powerful, or of noble birth. If, though, the Corinthians are now claiming to be wise etc., but concede they were not so at the time of their calling, this must imply that there has been a change: God has made the foolish wise, the weak have become strong, the poor have become rich.[61] But this is precisely the story line and the governing motif of the song of Hannah in 1 Kingdoms 2! The broader context in 1 Kingdoms 2.1–10 of the oracle cited in 1 Corinthians 1.31 and alluded to by Paul is precisely about the reversal of fortunes brought by God.[62] According to the song, God is the one who 'makes poor and *makes rich* [πλουτίζει]'

(v. 7 LXX), he 'raises the poor from the dust and makes them sit with rulers of peoples (δυναστῶν λαῶν) and makes them inherit a *throne of glory* [θρόνον δόξης]' (v. 8). Although, as many have pointed out, the language of the apparent claims of the Corinthians in 4.8, 10 can be paralleled in a wide range of sources, both Jewish and non-Jewish,[63] it is striking how much the slightly wider context of the oracle cited by Paul in 1 Corinthians 1.31, if taken from the version in 1 Kingdoms 2, seems to fit the *Corinthian* situation and self-understanding almost like a glove. Could it be then that the echoes of the fuller oracle, which do seem to be there in Paul's language in 1.26, may have been heard precisely because the oracle and its slightly wider context in 1 Kingdoms 2 (rather than Jeremiah 9) were already in the minds of Paul's readers/hearers as providing the basis for their own self-understanding?[64]

In general terms, the idea does not seem implausible. We have already seen that some knowledge of the Old Testament on the part of the Corinthians is not improbable. The possibility that the Corinthians might have sought to establish their beliefs on the basis of scripture may also be implied by Paul's words in 1 Corinthians 1.20, 'Where is the wise man? Where is the scribe? Where is the debater of this age?': the three nouns – σοφός, γραμματεύς, συζητητής – suggest work in interpreting scripture.[65] Hence the σοφία of the Corinthians may come, at least in part, from *their* use of scripture.[66]

Further, there is a bit of evidence for the use of the song of Hannah at this period. Pseudo-Phocylides 53 parallels the oracle of 1 Kingdoms 2.10/Jeremiah 9.22–3. Pseudo-Philo expands the song very considerably but also clearly knows the LXX version of 1 Kingdoms 2.10 (cf. Pseudo-Philo 50.2).[67] Within the early Christian tradition, we know too that the song was influential in providing the basis for the Magnificat of Luke 1. Some evidence from Philo may also be relevant here. A number of scholars have argued in recent years that the most important background for illuminating the Corinthians' ideas may be ideas about Wisdom in Hellenistic Judaism, especially as found in Philo.[68] It may then be significant that the song of Hannah is alluded to at a number of places by Philo. At one point Philo explicitly refers to Hannah as 'the gift of the wisdom of God' (*Quod Deus* 5). Elsewhere, on a number of occasions he refers explicitly to the verse in 1 Samuel 2.5 ('the barren hath borne seven'), interpreting the words variously of the soul free from passions (*Quod Deus* 10–15, *de Mutatione Nominum* 143–4; cf. too *de Praemiis et Poenis* 159–60, *de Ebrietate* 145–52). The use of the song of Hannah by Philo may then add some support to the theory that the Corinthians themselves had already appealed to this song to justify their own position as people who possessed true wisdom and who had been made 'rich', 'powerful', and able to sit on some kind of throne by God.

Paul's response is perhaps a little coded and guarded. Paul's exhortation is that one should 'boast in the Lord' but this κύριος is characterized by a cross. Paul's use of the oracle is thus strictly limited, and he almost seems to want to avoid any discussion of the wider context. Could this then be the force of Paul's (in)famous words in 1 Corinthians 4.6, where he tells the Corinthians not to (go) 'beyond what is written'? There is no time to rehearse here the various possibilities that have been proposed to explain Paul's highly enigmatic statement.[69] I am persuaded by the arguments of those who propose that ἃ γέγραπται here refers to Old Testament scripture, and that the scriptures concerned are probably the texts which Paul has cited thus far in the letter.[70] Nevertheless, the ὑπέρ here has always been problematic: in what sense should one not go 'beyond' what is written? Most of those who have wrestled with the problem acknowledge the difficulty, but often seem to end up effectively making the ὑπέρ mean 'against' so that Paul is simply made to say 'do not disobey' scripture.[71]

If, though, the situation in Corinth was as suggested above, then it may be that the Corinthians were 'going beyond' the texts actually cited by Paul by appealing to the broader context of, say, the song of Hannah to justify their own self-understanding. It is then Paul who may be somewhat uneasy about such a procedure. Paul wants the Corinthians to stick to what *he* has said, and to the form in which *he* has cited the scriptural texts to support his argument.[72] It could be, then, that the situation in 1 Corinthians 1—4 is not dissimilar to that in 1 Corinthians 15, where both Paul and the Corinthians are appealing to an earlier tradition (in 1 Corinthians 15 it is probably the primitive Christian kerygma) but drawing rather different conclusions from it.[73] The dispute is thus a hermeneutical one: how is one to interpret a tradition valued by both sides in a debate but giving rise to radically different interpretations? If the above suggestion is anywhere near the truth, Paul's argument seems to be to stick to individual texts, at times suitably adapted, and to go no further. If there are 'echoes' of scripture to be heard, in the sense of allusions to (only slightly) broader contexts, it may be the Corinthians who are more prepared to do this and Paul who sets his face (at least here) against such a procedure. Paul may thus be wanting to *limit* any appeal to wider contexts of scripture.

In any case Paul's appeal to scripture in this section may be less important than other factors in his overall argument. Far more central to Paul's argument here are the twin (or connected) appeals to the person of Jesus and to the figure of himself as an apostle as paradigms for Christian existence. Thus in 4.6 itself Paul says that he has applied the whole of the previous argument to himself and Apollos so that the Corinthians may learn what it means 'not to go beyond what is written': i.e. it is Paul and Apollos who provide the real criterion for determining how scripture is to be read. So too in the heavy irony of 4.8ff., it is Paul's own apostolic life which provides the counter to Corinthian claims about their status, their 'wealth' and their 'wisdom'. In 4.16, Paul explicitly says 'be imitators of me', and in 4.17 it is Paul's own 'ways in Christ Jesus' that the Corinthians are to be reminded of by Timothy. Earlier in the section it is the person of Jesus as the crucified one who provides the primary criterion for mounting the critique of the Corinthian claims about their σοφία: cf. the stress in chapter 1 on the cross as providing the true σοφία of God which undermines all other claims to wisdom. In 2.2 Paul states that he will have no other basis for his preaching than that of the crucified Jesus. And the wisdom that Paul will concede and accept for the mature (2.6–16) is the wisdom that comes from the mind of Christ (v. 16). It is the gospel of Christ crucified, and the claim that this gospel is exemplified in his own apostolic existence, that provides the fundamental basis for Paul's attempt to change the self-understanding of the Corinthians.[74] In all this, Old Testament scripture is occasionally cited but generally plays only a subsidiary role in the argument as a whole.

To say that Paul's ethic is primarily christocentric is scarcely very startling in terms of contemporary scholarship.[75] Nor is it very novel to say that the Old Testament plays a rather subsidiary role in Paul's ethic (though there has been a strong upsurge of support in recent years for the opposite view).[76] Rather, one could say that this study gives some support to the view of Barnabas Lindars, that it is Christology which is central for Paul and that the Old Testament is used primarily to back that up where appropriate.[77]

Notes

1 In general terms, see the early study of C. H. Dodd, *According to the Scriptures: The Sub-structure of New Testament Theology*, London, 1952. Many other, more recent studies could be cited, though space precludes naming them explicitly here. But pre-eminent in the contemporary debate has been the work of R. B. Hays, *Echoes of Scripture in the Letters of Paul* (New Haven

and London, 1989), and others developing insights from so-called 'intertextuality'. (And if my debate is primarily with Hays, this is simply a recognition of the programmatic significance of his work here.)

It is however doubtful whether this really should be described as 'intertextuality', at least insofar as that word is used by secular literary critics: see my 'Scripture and Q', in C. M. Tuckett (ed.), *The Scriptures in the Gospels* (BETL 131; Leuven, 1998), pp. 3–26, esp. pp. 4–6; also T. R. Hatina, 'Intertextuality and Historical Criticism in New Testament Studies: Is There a Relationship?', *Biblical Interpretation*, 7 (1999) pp. 28–43; M. Rese, 'Intertextualität: Ein Beispiel für Sinn und Unsinn "neuer" Methoden', in Tuckett (ed.), *The Scriptures in the Gospels*, pp. 431–9. It is noteworthy that, although Hays presented his work in *Echoes* using the words 'intertextuality' or 'intertextual' freely, he has more recently stated that he is prepared to surrender it: see his 'A Response to Critiques of *Echoes of Scripture in the Letters of Paul*', in C. A. Evans and J. A. Sanders (eds), *Paul and the Scriptures of Israel* (JSNTSup 83; Sheffield, 1993), pp. 70–96, on p. 81 (responding to W. S. Green): 'Nothing is at stake for me in the use of the term.'

2 I am fully aware that many of the first recipients will have been hearers rather than readers: see p. 74. However, I have kept the term 'reader' simply to avoid an over-cumbersome use of 'reader/hearer' on each occasion.

3 See J. M. G. Barclay, 'Thessalonica and Corinth: Social Contrasts in Pauline Christianity', *JSNT*, 47 (1992), pp. 49–74.

4 Cf. R. E. Watts, *Isaiah's New Exodus and Mark* (WUNT 2.88; Tübingen, 1997), pp. 29–45, with reference to the work of Ricoeur, Ellul and others.

5 Cf. R. A. Horsley, *1 Corinthians* (Nashville, 1998), p. 135.

6 Hays refers on several occasions to the work of M. Fishbane, *Biblical Interpretation in Ancient Israel*, Oxford, 1985: cf. his *Echoes*, p. 14; also his 'The Conversion of the Imagination: Scripture and Eschatology in 1 Corinthians', *NTS*, 45 (1999), pp. 391–412, on p. 393 and n. 5. However, Fishbane is seeking to analyse a slightly different phenomenon, viz. what he calls 'inner Biblical exegesis' (i.e. interpretation of earlier scripture in later passages in the Hebrew Bible itself). He explicitly excludes Paul and other early Christian texts from this because their claims about, and their relationship to, early Jewish scripture is rather different (p. 10). In any case it is not clear that the first readers of Paul can be compared so easily with the later readers of Jewish scripture interpreting earlier scriptural texts. Would Paul's letters have been regarded as having scriptural status?

7 See F. F. Bruce, *Bibical Exegesis in the Qumran Texts* (The Hague, 1959); also D. Juel, *Messianic Exegesis: Christological Interpretation of the Old Testament in Early Christianity* (Philadelphia, 1987), ch. 2; cf. too T. H. Lim, *Holy Scripture in the Qumran Commentaries and Pauline Letters* (Oxford, 1997), esp. ch. 7.

8 Hays proposes seven 'tests' or guidelines (*Echoes*, pp. 29–32 cf. pp. 53–62

above). On these, see the critique of S. E. Porter, 'The Use of the Old Testament in the New Testament: A Brief Comment on Method and Terminology', in C. A. Evans and J. A. Sanders (eds), *Early Christian Interpretation of the Scriptures of Israel* (JSNTSup 148; Sheffield, 1997) pp. 79–96.

9   Cf. Hays, 'Conversion of the Imagination', p. 392: 'Allusions and echoes are for those who have ears to hear'. Perhaps this is a good example of the kind of 'intertextual echo' which, for an audience of professional New Testament scholars, would be clearly heard: the quotation marks are almost unnecessary to indicate the allusion to Mark 4 (or is it Isaiah 6?!). But then equally, there is absolutely no intention in making this echo to try to evoke the wider context of Mark 4, as if only those with 'eyes to see' have been granted somehow the mystery of the Kingdom!

10 In both instances an extra mini-'introduction' (καὶ ὅτι in Luke, καὶ πάλιν in Hebrews) suggests that the New Testament author thought of the two as separate quotations.

11 Cf. Paul's use of verses from Isaiah 28: vv. 11–12 are cited in 1 Corinthians 14.21, v. 16 in Romans 9.33; or from Isaiah 29 – v. 10 is cited in Romans 11.8, v. 14 in 1 Corinthians 1.19. So too the same Old Testament text can be cited more than once by Paul, but in different ways: cf. Jeremiah 9.23/ 1 Kingdoms 2.10 LXX (see p. 82), cited in 1 Corinthians 1.31 and 2 Corinthians 10.17.

12 See H. Y. Gamble, *Books and Readers in the Early Church: A History of Early Christian Texts* (New Haven and London, 1995), pp. 2–10. The standard work on literacy is W. Harris, *Ancient Literacy* (Cambridge, 1989).

13 See, for example, the well-known studies of Pauline communities by G. Theissen, *The Social Setting of Pauline Christianity* (ET Edinburgh, 1982); W. A. Meeks, *The First Urban Christians* (New Haven and London, 1983); A. J. Malherbe, *Social Aspects of Early Christianity* (Philadelphia, 1983).

14 It is true that relatively soon the new Christian movement became extremely productive in terms of producing new literature (cf. Gamble, *Books*, pp. 93–108). But our evidence comes from the post-Pauline period; in any case we do not know how far such productivity was accompanied by any general increase in the level of literacy of Christian groups as a whole.

15 Cf. C. D. Stanley, 'The Social Environment of "Free"' Biblical Quotations in the New Testament', in Evans and Sanders (eds), *Early Christian Interpretation*, pp. 18–27; more generally, P. J. Achtemeier, 'Omne verbum sonat: The New Testament and the Oral Environment of Late Western Antiquity', *JBL*, 109 (1990), pp. 3–27.

16 D. M. Smith, 'The Pauline Literature', in D. A. Carson and H. G. M. Williamson (eds), *It Is Written. Scripture Citing Scripture: Essays in Honour of Barnabas Lindars* (Cambridge, 1988), pp. 265–91, on p. 280: 'The Bible was a collection of scrolls, not a single volume.' See too C. D. Stanley,

'Biblical Quotations as Rhetorical Devices in Paul's Letter to the Galatians', *SBL 1998 Seminar Papers* (Atlanta, 1998), pp. 700–30, on pp. 717f. It is now widely accepted that the beginnings of the use of the codex may well have been significantly affected by early Christians: see C. H. Roberts and T. C. Skeat, *The Birth of the Codex* (Oxford, 1983); Gamble, *Books*, pp. 42–81; G. N. Stanton, 'The Fourfold Gospel', *NTS*, 43 (1997), pp. 317–46, on pp. 336–41. But this is unlikely to have pre-dated Paul's letters.

17 Cf. Smith, 'The Pauline Literature', p. 280: the Jewish Bible (as scrolls, not as a single book) 'was possibly not accessible outside a synagogue'. On the costliness of books, cf. Gamble, *Books*, pp. 83–93; also Harris, *Literacy*, pp. 193–6, 224–5.

18 C. D. Stanley, 'The Rhetoric of Quotations: An Essay in Method', in Evans and Sanders (eds), *Early Christian Interpretation*, pp. 44–58, on p. 52f. (referring to the work of M. Sternberg); also Stanley, 'Biblical Quotations as Rhetorical Devices', p. 720.

19 Cf. the theories of M. L. Strauss, *The Davidic Messiah in Luke-Acts: The Promise and its Fulfilment in Lukan Christology* (JSNTSup 110; Sheffield, 1995), or Watts, *Isaiah's New Exodus*, which presuppose knowledge of, and cross-referencing within, texts as wide-ranging as the whole of the present book of Isaiah. On this, see my 'The Christology of Luke-Acts', in J. Verheyden (ed.), *The Unity of Luke-Acts* (BETL 142; Leuven, 1999), pp. 133–64, on p. 159.

20 Cf. n. 17 above.

21 Otherwise the assumption of so many Jewish beliefs and presuppositions, e.g. in the areas of theology (i.e. the idea of God), eschatology and ethics, by early Christian writers makes it very difficult to see how communication could have taken place.

22 Seeking to find parallels to the alleged practice of reading Jewish scripture in other Jewish groups of the period is one thing. But I find it difficult to accept that the use of allusive 'echoes' in English poetry is necessarily a good parallel to use for illuminating the way in which Paul's letters might have been read in the first century. Cf. Hays's indebtedness to the work of John Hollander, *The Figure of Echo: A Mode of Allusion in Milton and After* (Berkeley, 1981). Quite apart from the temporal problems of comparing much later texts with Paul's letters, there is the generic problem: Paul's letters are surely *mis*read if they are read as 'poetry' with all the interpretative presuppositions which we might bring to bear in reading what we regard as 'poetry'.

23 *Pace* Lim (especially if attention is focused on the *Pesharim* commentaries): see the review of Lim's book by C. D. Stanley in *JTS*, 49 (1998), pp. 781–4.

24 See however the caveats expressed (in general terms) in the important recent article of C. D. Stanley, '"Pearls Before Swine": Did Paul's Audiences Understand His Biblical Quotations?', *NovT*, 41 (1999) pp.

124–44. Stanley offers many general arguments against the theory that Paul's audiences understood much if anything of his references to scripture, let alone were sensitive to unquoted parts of broader contexts. He warns against 'the kind of "mirror-reading" that assumes we can discover what Paul's addressees knew about the Jewish Scriptures by studying how Paul himself interprets the biblical text' (p. 136, cf. too p. 124).

As will have been evident, I am very sympathetic to Stanley's overall approach and have learnt much from this and all his writings (as the footnotes make clear; his most recent article reached me after the present essay was already in draft form). Nevertheless Stanley makes little of the variation in Paul's use of scripture between different letters. Such variation might reasonably suggest that Paul at least *thought* that some of his readers were more 'attuned' to hearing Old Testament quotations than others. And if we are to be sensitive to the potential *variety* between and within Pauline communities in this respect (as we surely should be), then perhaps Paul's own use of scripture may not be wholly irrelevant.

25 Cf. G. D. Fee, *The First Epistle to the Corinthians* (Grand Rapids, 1987), p. 443: 'The nature of the following argument [in 10.1–13] suggests that they [the Corinthians] were well aware of the data of the text.'

26 The equation is made by Philo, *Legum Allegoria* 2.86. See C. K. Barrett, *The First Epistle to the Corinthians* (London, 1968), p. 222; H. Conzelmann, *1 Corinthians* (ET Philadelphia, 1975), p. 167; and many others.

27 For further evidence of some familiarity on the part of the Corinthians with the Old Testament, see 1 Corinthians 15, where Paul indulges in some detailed arguments based on the Old Testament (cf. esp. vv. 24–8); also, if 2 Corinthians is relevant, there is Paul's use of the story of Exodus 34 in 2 Corinthians 3 (see p. 8 above).

28 Cf. too 1 Corinthians 6.10–11, 8.7 (some were idolaters – hardly language appropriate to Jews). Cf. Fee, *First Epistle*, p. 4. I am assuming throughout this paper that the addressees in 1 Corinthians form a unified single group. I am fully aware that this is disputed, but there is no space here to debate the issue.

29 On this see A. Lindemann, 'Die paulinische Ekklesiologie angesichts der Lebenswirklichkeit der christlichen Gemeinde in Korinth', in R. Bieringer(ed.), *The Corinthian Correspondence* (BETL 125; Leuven, 1996) pp. 63–86, esp. pp. 67f. For the basic reliability of the account in Acts here, see G. Lüdemann, *Early Christianity according to the Traditions in Acts* (ET London, 1987) pp. 201–4.

30 This is of course a typical Lukan feature; but that does not make it *ipso facto* unhistorical.

31 There is no space here to enter the vexed debate about the existence of a specific group of 'God-fearers' in Judaism at this period. See the discussion in M. C. de Boer, 'God-Fearers in Luke-Acts', in C. M. Tuckett (ed.),

Luke's Literary Achievement (JSNTSup 116; Sheffield, 1995), pp. 50–71.
32 Deuteronomy 13.5, 17.7, 19.19, 22.21, 22, 24, 24.7.
33 Cf. E. E. Ellis, *Paul's Use of the Old Testament* (Grand Rapids, 1957); D.-A. Koch, *Die Schrift als Zeuge des Evangeliums: Untersuchungen zur Verwendung und zum Verhältnis der Schrift bei Paulus* (BHT 69; Tübingen, 1986); C. D. Stanley, *Paul and the Language of Scripture* (SNTSMS 74; Cambridge, 1992). Others are cited in B. S. Rosner, *Paul, Scripture and Ethics: A Study of 1 Corinthians 5—7* (AGAJU 22; Leiden, 1994), pp. 61–2.
34 Rosner, *Paul, Scripture and Ethics*, ch. 3. In his earlier work Hays argued that the allusion was to Deuteronomy 17.7 (*Echoes*, 97); in his more recent essay, Hays has moved slightly to seeing it as an allusion to Deuteronomy 22, partly under the influence of the work of Rosner: see Hays, 'Conversion of the Imagination', pp. 410–11 and nn. 45, 47.
35 In Deuteronomy 22.22 it is in relation to a man having sexual relations with the wife of any other man. According to W. Horbury, 'Extirpation and Excommunication', *VT,* 35 (1985) pp. 13–38, these commands, originally referring to execution, were widely interpreted later as implying exclusion and expulsion from the community.
36 On the importance of some kind of 'marker' that a quotation is being given, at least for Paul's *audiences*, see Stanley, '"Pearls Before Swine"', pp. 132–3.
37 Rosner, *Paul*, pp. 65–81.
38 Rosner, *Paul*, p. 69, referring to D. Prior, *The Message of 1 Corinthians* (Leicester, 1985), p. 85; P. Ellingworth and H. Hatton, *A Translator's Guide on Paul's First Letter to the Corinthians* (London, 1985), p. 105.
39 See Rosner, *Paul*, pp. 71–3.
40 Though any idea of 'corporate personality' needs to be handled with some care: see J. W. Rogerson, 'The Hebrew Conception of Corporate Personality: A Re-examination', *JTS*, 21 (1970), pp. 1–16.
41 Whatever that implies. There is no space to discuss the issue here.
42 See too A. Y. Collins, 'The Function of "Excommunication" in Paul', *HTR*, 73 (1980), pp. 251–63. The Passover references which follow also suggest that an idea of holiness is in mind.
43 See L. E. Keck, 'Re-thinking "New Testament Ethics"', *JBL,* 115 (1996) pp. 3–16, on p. 8, for the importance of taking seriously what the authors themselves say in their justification for moral decisions. Contrast e.g. the argument of T. Holtz, 'The Question of the Content of Paul's Instruction', in B. Rosner (ed.), *Understanding Paul's Ethics* (Carlisle, 1995), pp. 51–71 (German original in *TLZ*, 106 (1981), pp. 385–400) on p. 55, who claims that the real reason for Paul's demand to the Corinthians not to frequent brothels cannot have been what he actually says in 1 Corinthians 6, since this would exclude all sexual relations: hence the real reason must be found somewhere else (i.e. in the Old Testament and Jewish tradition). Perhaps one should 'let Paul be Paul' (and 'let the reader understand' the 'intertextual' echoes!).

44 There is not enough space here to discuss the complicated problem of the precise syntax of vv. 3–4: see all the commentaries.
45 See H. D. Betz, *Galatians* (Philadelphia, 1979), p. 266 for references.
46 See J. Jeremias, *The Eucharistic Words of Jesus* (ET London, 1966), p. 60, who refers to the sudden change to the first person, as well as some Semitic and un-Pauline elements in the language used here.
47 πονηρία might be seen as a word play on πορνεία (cf. P. Zaas, 'Cast Out the Evil Man from Your Midst", *JBL*, 103 (1984), pp. 259–61, on p. 259), but if so it is not clear why any word play was felt to be needed at all.
48 Cf. too Conzelmann, *1 Corinthians*, p. 48; Fee, *First Epistle*, p. 218: Paul 'clearly assumes that his Gentile readers will understand this thoroughly Jewish image'. It is notable that Philo interprets the Passover in allegorical terms in *Quaest.Exod.* 1.4; and in 1.15 he too interprets the leavened/unleavened bread in ethical terms: 'Such [leavened/unleavened bread] is a symbol of types of soul, one [leavened] being haughty and swollen with arrogance, the other [unleavened] being unchangeable and prudent . . . . We eat the opposite of overboastful arrogance through meditation on humility, which is called reverence.' See p. 85 for the possible importance of Philo's writings for illuminating the background of the Corinthians' thought and ideology.
49 J. Ross Wagner, '"Not Beyond the Things which are Written": A Call to Boast only in the Lord (1 Cor 4.6)', *NTS*, 44 (1998), pp. 279–87.
50 The versions differ slightly at the end: Jeremiah 9.24 MT has 'knows me, that I am the Lord who practises kindness, justice'. Jeremiah 9.23 LXX has 'knows that I am the Lord who practises mercy, justice'; 1 Kingdoms 2.10 LXX has 'knows the Lord, and practises justice'. The differences between the two versions do not affect the issue here.
51 Paul deletes any mention of activity by the human subject in the boasting: one is simply to boast 'in the Lord': one does not oneself 'understand' or 'know', let alone actually 'practise' the justice etc. as in the 1 Kingdoms 2 version.
52 See G. O'Day, 'Jeremiah 9:22–23 and 1 Cor 1:26–31: A Study in Intertextuality', *JBL*, 109 (1990), pp. 259–67; R. B. Hays, 'The Role of Scripture in Paul's Ethics', in E. H. Lovering and J. L. Sumney (eds), *Theology and Ethics in Paul and his Interpreters: Essays in Honor of Victor Paul Furnish* (Nashville, 1996), pp. 30–47 on p. 44; also his 'Conversion of the Imagination', pp. 405–6; Wagner, 'Not Beyond', passim. Although much has been made in terms of 'intertextuality' as illuminating Paul's procedure here, the suggestion that Jeremiah 9 lies behind more than just v. 31 of the passage had been made well before 'intertextuality' became such an in-word in New Testament studies: cf. Barrett, *First Epistle*, pp. 51–61; also Fee, *First Epistle*, p. 78.
53 This is the usual interpretation of the verse (and has of course given rise to

many conclusions about the social setting of the Corinthian community). However, in seeking to reinforce the theory that the full oracle (of Jeremiah 9) is in mind, Gail O'Day has defended an alternative reading of the verse, taking up an earlier suggestion by W. Wuellner about v. 26: rather than being an indicative statement about the position of the Corinthians, v. 26 should be taken as a series of questions expecting the answer 'yes' – 'Were not many of you wise? Were not many of you powerful?' – to which the implied answer is 'yes indeed we were/are' (W. Wuellner, 'The Sociological Implications of 1 Corinthians 1:26–28 Reconsidered', *SE*, 6 (*TU*, 112; Berlin, 1973)), pp. 666–72, on pp. 668–9; O'Day, 'Jeremiah 9:22–23', pp. 263–5.) On the more usual reading of v. 26, it is the actual situation of the Corinthian community that inverts the world's values and shames others, yet this is 'theologically dubious, because for Paul it is the cross, not the divided and divisive Corinthian community, that shames the world' (p. 265).

Such a reading does not, however, seem persuasive. First, Paul is not claiming that it is the 'divided and divisive Corinthian community' as such that shames the world. No doubt for Paul it is ultimately the cross that shames the world. But the point of his argument in vv. 27–8 is that there is some positive correlation between the cross and aspects of those whom God has chosen in that all serve to invert the world's values. Second, it is hard to believe that Paul's addressees are not included (by Paul) in the list in vv. 27–8. In the introductory βλέπετε γὰρ τὴν κλῆσιν ὑμῶν, the γάρ suggests that the appeal to Corinthians to 'consider their calling' will positively support Paul's general claim in v. 25 about the superiority of divine folly/wisdom and weakness/strength over human wisdom and power. O'Day's reading implies a contrast between the situation of the addressees and Paul's claims. But the γάρ in v. 26 suggests that the appeal to the Corinthians' position supports, rather than works against, Paul's argument. The alternative reading of v. 26 would have to assume that the foolish/weak/no-accounts who have been chosen by God (vv. 27–8) are precisely *not* the Corinthian addressees. However, Paul says in v. 30 that it is 'you' – not 'they' or 'others' – who have their origin in the God who has called all these 'nobodies'. The implication is that those addressed are among the foolish/weak etc. and also that they acknowledge the fact. Otherwise the rhetoric of the argument never gets off the ground. Cf. too the discussion of the reference to 'noble birth' above: Paul is proposing a negative statement with which the Corinthians will agree.

54 Paul's δυνατός is also not quite identical to Jeremiah's ἰσχυρός, although Paul uses ἰσχυρός in v. 27 and in any case the two words are close in meaning if not exactly synonymous.
55 See Meeks, *First Urban Christians*.
56 See too Fee, *First Epistle*, p. 80. Paul would presumably not want them to agree that they were 'poor' when he appeals to them for money (cf. 16.1)!

57 Hays, 'Conversion of the Imagination', p. 405.
58 On the importance of 'markers' indicating a quotation, at least for audiences, cf. n. 36 above.
59 I am aware that this might be illegitimately equating Paul's 'implied readers' with his real readers (cf. Stanley, "Pearls Before Swine", *passim*). On the other hand, Stanley himself concedes that the general situation would be significantly different if the audience already knew the Old Testament texts being alluded to or cited (cf. pp. 130, 132). What follows is admittedly a little speculative, but perhaps worth exploring as a possibility.
60 So Conzelmann, *1 Corinthians*, p. 49; Barrett, *First Epistle*, p. 51; Fee, *First Epistle*, p. 79.
61 It is noteworthy that 'rich' does appear in 4.8, unlike 1.26: cf. above.
62 Wagner, 'Not Beyond', p. 284, claims that the song 'resounds from start to finish with the theme of the reversal *of human pride*' (my stress), and hence regards the whole song as meshing in with *Paul's* argument. More apt seems to be Hays's characterization: 'a song that extols God for having reversed the fortunes of the poor and the downtrodden' ('Conversion of the Imagination', p. 405, though Hays himself follows Wagner as seeing this as fitting Paul's argument). In fact, in trying to find any resonance between Paul and the wider song, Hays can only refer to one verse in the song, viz. v. 3: 'do not boast, and do not speak lofty things; do not let grandiloquence [μεγαλορρημοσύνη] come out of your mouth' (cf. too his 'Role of Scripture', p. 44).
63 See Conzelmann, *1 Corinthians*, pp. 87–8; D. W. Kuck, *Judgment and Community Conflict: Paul's Use of Apocalyptic Judgment Language in 1 Corinthians 3:5—4:5* (NovTSup 66; Leiden, 1992) pp. 217–18. Relevant also may be the parallels in the Jesus tradition of the beatitudes.
64 Stanley, 'Biblical Quotations as Rhetorical Devices', pp. 704–5, points out that one of the rhetorical functions which quotations can serve is the establishment of common ground between the two parties involved in the communication process. (Stanley's essay is an excellent study of the way in which quotations can and do actually *function* within discourse.) Cf. too D.-A. Koch, 'Schriftauslegung II', *TRE*, 30.2.3 (1999), p. 458.
65 See J. A. Davis, *Wisdom and Spirit* (New York, 1984), p. 73, referring to N. A. Dahl, 'Paul and the Church at Corinth according to 1 Corinthians 1.10—4.21', in W. R. Farmer *et al.* (eds), *Christian History and Interpretation* (Cambridge, 1967), pp. 313–35, on p. 328, and others; cf. too Fee, *First Epistle*, pp. 70–1.
66 Thus agreeing in part with M. D. Goulder, 'Σοφία in 1 Corinthians', *NTS*, 37 (1991), pp. 516–34, though I have difficulty with other aspects of his theories: see my 'Jewish Christian Wisdom in 1 Corinthians?', in S. E. Porter *et al.* (eds), *Crossing the Boundaries. Essays in Biblical Interpretation in Honour of Michael D. Goulder* (Leiden, 1994), pp. 201–20.

67 Cf. P.-M. Bogaert, 'Luc et les écritures dans l'évangile de l'enfance à la lumière des "Antiquités Bibliques": Histoire sainte et livres saints', in Tuckett (ed.), *The Scriptures in the Gospels*, pp. 243–70, on pp. 259–60.
68 See B. Pearson, *The Pneumatikos–Psychikos Terminology in 1 Corinthians* (Missoula, Mont., 1973); R. A. Horsley, 'Pneumatikos versus Psychikos: Distinctions of Status among the Corinthians', *HTR*, 69 (1976), pp. 269–88, 'Wisdom of Word and Words of Wisdom', *CBQ*, 39 (1977), pp. 224–39; '"How Can Some of You Say that there is No Resurrection of the Dead?": Spiritual Elitism in Corinth', *NovT*, 20 (1978), pp. 203–31; also his *1 Corinthians*, p. 35; Davis, *Wisdom and Spirit*. Cf. too n. 48 above on Philo's ethical interpretation of 'leaven' and 'unleaven'.
69 Many are covered in Wagner, 'Not Beyond', passim. See too Hays, 'Conversion of the Imagination', pp. 407–8, n. 40, for discussion and (in my view justified) critique of two recent studies, viz. R. L Tyler, 'First Corinthians 4:6 and Hellenistic Pedagogy', *CBQ*, 60 (1998), pp. 97–103, and J. C. Hanges, '1 Corinthians 4:6 and the Possibility of Written Bylaws in the Corinthian Church', *JBL*, 117 (1998), pp. 275–98.
70 See especially Wagner, 'Not Beyond', developing the earlier study of M. D. Hooker, '"Beyond the Things Which Are Written": An Examination of 1 Cor. IV.6', *NTS*, 10 (1963), pp. 127–32, repr. in her *From Adam to Christ: Essays on Paul* (Cambridge, 1990), pp. 106–12.
71 Cf. Hooker, *From Adam to Christ*, p. 109; also Wagner, 'Not Beyond', p. 280: 'As a positive command it [1.31] is liable to transgression, and so the exhortation not to "go beyond" the command makes sense' (apparently equating 'going beyond' with 'transgression'). See also Hays, 'Conversion of the Imagination', pp. 406–7: 'It [1 Corinthians 4.6] means that Paul is trying to teach the puffed-up Corinthians not to *transgress* the specific scriptural warnings against arrogance' (my stress).
72 Cf. too 1 Corinthians 3.20, where Paul cites Psalm 94.11, but where he changes the psalm's original ἀνθρώπων to σοφῶν, almost certainly to suit his own argument and claims (cf. Stanley, *Paul and the Language of Scripture*, pp. 194–5).
73 See my 'The Corinthians Who Say "There is No Resurrection of the Dead"', in R. Bieringer, *The Corinthian Correspondence* (BETL 125; Leuven, 1996), pp. 247–75; also J. H. Schütz, *Paul and the Anatomy of Apostolic Authority* (SNTSMS 26; Cambridge, 1975) pp. 84–113.
74 For the idea that the apostolic life exemplifies the gospel, see especially Schütz, *Paul and the Anatomy*; also G. Lyons, *Pauline Autobiography* (SBLDS 73; Atlanta, 1985); B. Gaventa, 'Galatians 1 and 2: Autobiography as Paradigm', *NovT*, 28 (1986), pp. 309–26; B. Dodd, *Paul's Paradigmatic 'I': Personal Example as Literary Strategy* (JSNTSup 177; Sheffield, 1999).
75 Cf. Keck, 'Rethinking', p. 10; R. B. Hays, *The Moral Vision of the New Testament* (New York, 1996), pp. 27–32; D. G. Horrell, 'Theological

Principle or Christological Praxis? Pauline Ethics in 1 Corinthians 8.1–11.1', *JSNT*, 67 (1997), pp. 83–114, and many others.

76 See the classic essay of A. von Harnack, 'The Old Testament in the Pauline Letters and in the Pauline Churches', ET in B. Rosner (ed.), *Understanding Paul's Ethics* (Carlisle, 1995), pp. 27–49 (German original 1928). For a fuller list of those who have down-played the role of scripture in Paul's ethics, see Rosner, *Paul*, p. 4 (though of course Rosner himself would wish to argue against such a position). For the contrary view, cf. the recent studies of Hays and Rosner, as well as the work of scholars such as P. Tomson, M. Bockmuehl and K. Finsterbusch.

77 See Barnabas Lindars, 'The Place of the Old Testament in the Formation of New Testament Theology', *NTS*, 23 (1976), pp. 59–66, on p. 66.

Index of Old Testament Quotations in New Testament Passages

OT quotation	Version	NT passage	
Genesis 1.26		James	3.9
Genesis 1.27		Matthew	19.4
Genesis 1.27		Mark	10.6
Genesis 2.2		Hebrews	4.4
Genesis 2.7		1 Corinthians	15.45
Genesis 2.24		Matthew	19.5
Genesis 2.24		Mark	10.7–8
Genesis 2.24		1 Corinthians	6.16
Genesis 2.24		Ephesians	5.31
Genesis 5.2		Matthew	19.4
Genesis 5.2		Mark	10.6
Genesis 5.24	LXX	Hebrews	11.5
Genesis 12.1		Acts	7.3
Genesis 12.3		Acts	3.25
Genesis 12.3		Galatians	3.8
Genesis 12.7		Galatians	3.16
Genesis 13.15		Galatians	3.16
Genesis 14.17–20		Hebrews	7.1–2
Genesis 15.5		Romans	4.18
Genesis 15.5		Hebrews	11.12
Genesis 15.6		Romans	4.3, 9, 22
Genesis 15.6		Galatians	3.6
Genesis 15.6		James	2.23
Genesis 15.13–14		Acts	7.6–7
Genesis 17.5		Romans	4.17, 18
Genesis 17.7		Galatians	3.16
Genesis 17.8		Acts	7.5

INDEX OF OLD TESTAMENT QUOTATIONS

OT quotation	Version	NT passage	
Genesis 17.8		Galatians	3.16
Genesis 18.10, 14		Romans	9.9
Genesis 18.18		Acts	3.25
Genesis 18.18		Galatians	3.8
Genesis 21.10		Galatians	4.30
Genesis 21.12		Romans	9.7
Genesis 21.12		Hebrews	11.18
Genesis 22.9		James	2.21
Genesis 22.16–17		Hebrews	6.13–14
Genesis 22.17		Hebrews	11.12
Genesis 22.18		Acts	3.25
Genesis 22.18		Galatians	3.8, 16
Genesis 25.23		Romans	9.12
Genesis 26.3–4		Acts	3.25
Genesis 26.3–4		Galatians	3.8, 16
Genesis 28.12		John	1.51
Genesis 28.13–14		Acts	3.25
Genesis 28.13–14		Galatians	3.8
Genesis 47.31	LXX	Hebrews	11.21
Genesis 48.4		Acts	7.5
Exodus 1.8		Acts	7.18
Exodus 2.11–15		Acts	7.23–9
Exodus 2.14		Acts	7.27–8, 35
Exodus 3.2		Acts	7.3
Exodus 3.5–10		Acts	7.32–4
Exodus 3.6		Matthew	22.32
Exodus 3.6		Mark	12.26
Exodus 3.6		Luke	20.37
Exodus 3.6		Acts	3.13
Exodus 3.6		Acts	7.32
Exodus 3.12		Acts	7.7
Exodus 3.15		Matthew	22.32
Exodus 3.15		Mark	12.26
Exodus 3.15		Luke	20.37
Exodus 3.15		Acts	3.13, 7.32
Exodus 9.16	LXX	Romans	9.17

INDEX OF OLD TESTAMENT QUOTATIONS

OT quotation		Version	NT passage	
Exodus	12.46		John	19.36
Exodus	13.2		Luke	2.23
Exodus	13.12		Luke	2.23
Exodus	13.15		Luke	2.32
Exodus	16.4		John	6.31
Exodus	16.18		2 Corinthians	8.15
Exodus	19.5–6	LXX	1 Peter	2.9
Exodus	19.12–13		Hebrews	12.20
Exodus	20.12–16		Matthew	19.18–19
Exodus	20.12–16		Mark	10.19
Exodus	20.12–16		Luke	18.30
Exodus	20.12		Matthew	15.4
Exodus	20.12		Mark	7.10
Exodus	20.12		Ephesians	6.2–3
Exodus	20.13–15, 17		Romans	13.9
Exodus	20.13–14		James	2.11
Exodus	20.13		Matthew	5.21
Exodus	20.14		Matthew	5.27
Exodus	20.17		Romans	7.7
Exodus	21.17		Matthew	15.4
Exodus	21.17		Mark	7.10
Exodus	21.24		Matthew	5.38
Exodus	22.28		Acts	23.5
Exodus	24.8		Hebrews	9.20
Exodus	25.40		Hebrews	8.5
Exodus	32.1		Acts	7.40
Exodus	32.6		1 Corinthians	10.7
Exodus	32.23		Acts	7.40
Exodus	33.19		Romans	9.15
Exodus	34.30		2 Corinthians	3.7
Exodus	34.33, 35		2 Corinthians	3.13
Exodus	34.34		2 Corinthians	3.16
Leviticus	2.13		Mark	9.49
Leviticus	11.44–5		1 Peter	1.16
Leviticus	12.6–8		Luke	2.24
Leviticus	16.27		Hebrews	13.11

INDEX OF OLD TESTAMENT QUOTATIONS

OT quotation	Version	NT passage	
Leviticus 18.5		Romans	10.5
Leviticus 18.5		Galatians	3.12
Leviticus 19.2		1 Peter	1.16
Leviticus 19.12		Matthew	5.33
Leviticus 19.18		Matthew	5.43
Leviticus 19.18		Matthew	19.19
Leviticus 19.18		Matthew	22.39
Leviticus 19.18		Mark	12.31, 33
Leviticus 19.18		Luke	10.27
Leviticus 19.18		Romans	13.9
Leviticus 19.18		Galatians	5.14
Leviticus 19.18		James	2.8
Leviticus 24.20		Matthew	5.38
Leviticus 26.12		2 Corinthians	6.16
Numbers 9.12		John	19.36
Numbers 12.7		Hebrews	3.2, 5
Numbers 16.5		2 Timothy	2.19
Numbers 27.17		Matthew	9.36
Numbers 27.17		Mark	6.34
Numbers 30.2		Matthew	5.33
Deuteronomy 4.24		Hebrews	12.29
Deuteronomy 4.35		Mark	12.32
Deuteronomy 5.16–20		Matthew	19.18–19
Deuteronomy 5.16–20		Mark	10.19
Deuteronomy 5.16–20		Luke	18.20
Deuteronomy 5.16		Matthew	15.4
Deuteronomy 5.16		Mark	7.10
Deuteronomy 5.16		Ephesians	6.2–3
Deuteronomy 5.17–19, 21		Romans	13.9
Deuteronomy 5.17–18		James	2.11
Deuteronomy 5.17		Matthew	5.21
Deuteronomy 5.18		Matthew	5.27
Deuteronomy 5.21		Romans	7.7
Deuteronomy 6.4–5		Mark	12.29–30

INDEX OF OLD TESTAMENT QUOTATIONS

OT quotation		Version	NT passage	
Deuteronomy	6.4–5		Mark	12.32–3
Deuteronomy	6.5		Matthew	22.37
Deuteronomy	6.5		Luke	10.27
Deuteronomy	6.13		Matthew	4.10
Deuteronomy	6.13		Luke	4.8
Deuteronomy	6.16		Matthew	4.7
Deuteronomy	6.16		Luke	4.12
Deuteronomy	8.3		Matthew	4.4
Deuteronomy	8.3		Luke	4.4
Deuteronomy	9.4		Romans	10.6
Deuteronomy	9.19		Hebrews	12.21
Deuteronomy	17.6		Hebrews	10.28
Deuteronomy	17.7	LXX	1 Corinthians	5.13
Deuteronomy	18.15–19		Acts	3.22–3
Deuteronomy	18.15		Acts	7.37
Deuteronomy	19.15		Matthew	18.16
Deuteronomy	19.15		John	8.17
Deuteronomy	19.15		2 Corinthians	13.1
Deuteronomy	19.15		1 Timothy	5.19
Deuteronomy	19.19		1 Corinthians	5.13
Deuteronomy	19.21		Matthew	5.38
Deuteronomy	21.23		Galatians	3.13
Deuteronomy	22.21, 24		1 Corinthians	5.13
Deuteronomy	24.1		Matthew	5.31
Deuteronomy	24.1		Matthew	19.7
Deuteronomy	24.1, 3		Mark	10.4
Deuteronomy	24.7		1 Corinthians	5.13
Deuteronomy	25.4		1 Corinthians	9.9
Deuteronomy	25.4		1 Timothy	5.18
Deuteronomy	25.5		Matthew	22.24
Deuteronomy	25.5		Mark	12.19
Deuteronomy	25.5		Luke	20.28
Deuteronomy	27.26	LXX	Galatians	3.10
Deuteronomy	29.4		Romans	11.8
Deuteronomy	29.18		Hebrews	12.15
Deuteronomy	30.12–14		Romans	10.6–8
Deuteronomy	31.6, 8		Hebrews	13.5
Deuteronomy	32.17		1 Corinthians	10.20

INDEX OF OLD TESTAMENT QUOTATIONS

OT quotation	Version	NT passage	
Deuteronomy 32.21		Romans	10.19
Deuteronomy 32.21		1 Corinthians	10.22
Deuteronomy 32.35		Romans	12.19
Deuteronomy 32.35		Hebrews	10.30
Deuteronomy 32.36		Hebrews	10.30
Deuteronomy 32.43		Romans	15.10
Deuteronomy 32.43	LXX	Hebrews	1.6
Joshua 1.5		Hebrews	13.5
1 Samuel 2.1		Luke	1.46–7
1 Samuel 2.26		Luke	2.52
1 Samuel 13.14		Acts	13.22
2 Samuel 7.8, 14		2 Corinthians	6.18
2 Samuel 7.12–13		Acts	2.3
2 Samuel 7.14		Hebrews	1.5
2 Samuel 22.5		Romans	15.9
1 Kings 19.10, 14		Romans	11.3
1 Kings 19.18		Romans	11.4
1 Kings 22.17		Matthew	9.36
1 Kings 22.17		Mark	6.34
2 Kings 1.10, 12		Luke	9.54
2 Chronicles 18.16		Matthew	9.36
2 Chronicles 18.16		Mark	6.34
Nehemiah 9.15		John	6.31

INDEX OF OLD TESTAMENT QUOTATIONS

OT quotation	Version	NT passage	
Job 5.13		1 Corinthians	3.19
Job 41.11		Romans	11.35
Psalm 2.1–2	LXX	Acts	4.25–6
Psalm 2.7		Mark	1.11
Psalm 2.7		Luke	3.22
Psalm 2.7		Acts	13.33
Psalm 2.7		Hebrews	1.5
Psalm 2.7		Hebrews	5.5
Psalm 2.8–9		Revelation	2.26–7
Psalm 4.4	LXX	Ephesians	4.26
Psalm 5.9	LXX	Romans	3.13
Psalm 8.3	LXX	Matthew	21.26
Psalm 8.4–6	LXX	Hebrews	2.6–8
Psalm 8.6		1 Corinthians	15.27
Psalm 8.6		Ephesians	1.22
Psalm 10.7	LXX	Romans	3.14
Psalm 14.1–3		Romans	3.10–12
Psalm 16.8–11	LXX	Acts	2.25–8
Psalm 16.10		Acts	2.31
Psalm 16.10	LXX	Acts	13.35
Psalm 18.49		Romans	15.9
Psalm 19.4	LXX	Romans	10.18
Psalm 22.1		Matthew	27.46
Psalm 22.1		Mark	15.34
Psalm 22.7		Matthew	27.39
Psalm 22.7		Mark	15.29
Psalm 22.7		Luke	23.35
Psalm 22.8		Matthew	27.43
Psalm 22.18		Matthew	27.35
Psalm 22.18		Mark	15.24
Psalm 22.18		Luke	23.34
Psalm 22.18		John	19.24
Psalm 22.22		Hebrews	2.12
Psalm 24.1		1 Corinthians	10.26
Psalm 31.5		Luke	23.46
Psalm 32.1–2		Romans	4.7–8

INDEX OF OLD TESTAMENT QUOTATIONS

OT quotation	Version	NT passage	
Psalm 34.8		1 Peter	2.3
Psalm 34.12–16		1 Peter	3.10–12
Psalm 34.20		John	19.36
Psalm 35.19		John	15.25
Psalm 36.1		Romans	3.18
Psalm 37.11		Matthew	5.5
Psalm 40.6–8		Hebrews	10.5–7
Psalm 41.9		John	13.18
Psalm 44.22		Romans	8.36
Psalm 45.6–7		Hebrews	1.8–9
Psalm 48.2		Matthew	5.35
Psalm 51.4	LXX	Romans	3.4
Psalm 53.1–3		Romans	3.10–12
Psalm 68.18		Ephesians	4.8
Psalm 69.4		John	15.25
Psalm 69.9		John	2.17
Psalm 69.9		Romans	15.3
Psalm 69.21		Matthew	27.48
Psalm 69.21		Mark	15.36
Psalm 69.21		John	19.28–9
Psalm 69.22–3	LXX	Romans	11.9–10
Psalm 69.25		Acts	1.20
Psalm 78.2		Matthew	13.35
Psalm 78.24		John	6.31
Psalm 82.6		John	10.34
Psalm 90.4		2 Peter	3.8
Psalm 91.11–12		Matthew	4.6
Psalm 91.11–12		Luke	4.10–11
Psalm 94.11		1 Corinthians	3.20
Psalm 94.14		Romans	11.2
Psalm 95.7–11		Hebrews	3.7–11
Psalm 95.7–8	LXX	Hebrews	3.15
Psalm 95.7–8		Hebrews	4.7
Psalm 95.11		Hebrews	3.18
Psalm 95.11		Hebrews	4.3, 5, 10
Psalm 102.25–7	LXX	Hebrews	1.10–12
Psalm 103.8		James	5.11
Psalm 103.17		Luke	1.50

INDEX OF OLD TESTAMENT QUOTATIONS

OT quotation	Version	NT passage	
Psalm 104.4	LXX	Hebrews	1.7
Psalm 109.8		Acts	1.20
Psalm 110.1		Matthew	22.44
Psalm 110.1		Matthew	26.64
Psalm 110.1		Mark	12.36
Psalm 110.1		Mark	14.62
Psalm 110.1		Mark	16.19
Psalm 110.1		Luke	20.42–3
Psalm 110.1		Luke	22.69
Psalm 110.1		Acts	2.34–5
Psalm 110.1		1 Corinthians	15.25
Psalm 110.1		Ephesians	1.2
Psalm 110.1		Colossians	3.1
Psalm 110.1		Hebrews	1.3, 13
Psalm 110.1		Hebrews	8.1
Psalm 110.1		Hebrews	10.12–13
Psalm 110.1		Hebrews	12.2
Psalm 110.4		Hebrews	5.6
Psalm 110.4		Hebrews	7.17, 21
Psalm 112.9		2 Corinthians	9.9
Psalm 116.10	LXX	2 Corinthians	4.13
Psalm 117.1		Romans	15.11
Psalm 118.6	LXX	Hebrews	13.6
Psalm 118.22–3		Matthew	21.42
Psalm 118.22–3		Mark	12.10–11
Psalm 118.22–3		Luke	20.17
Psalm 118.22		Acts	4.11
Psalm 118.22		1 Peter	2.7
Psalm 118.25–6		Matthew	21.9
Psalm 118.25–6		Mark	11.9
Psalm 118.25–6		John	12.13
Psalm 118.26		Matthew	23.39
Psalm 118.26		Luke	13.35
Psalm 118.26		Luke	19.38
Psalm 132.11		Acts	2.30
Psalm 135.14		Hebrews	10.30
Psalm 140.3	LXX	Romans	3.13
Psalm 143.2		Romans	3.20

INDEX OF OLD TESTAMENT QUOTATIONS

OT quotation	Version	NT passage	
Proverbs 3.4		2 Corinthians	8.21
Proverbs 3.11–12	LXX	Hebrews	12.5–6
Proverbs 3.12		Revelation	3.19
Proverbs 3.34	LXX	James	4.6
Proverbs 3.34		1 Peter	5.5
Proverbs 4.26		Hebrews	12.13
Proverbs 10.12		1 Peter	4.8
Proverbs 11.31	LXX	1 Peter	4.18
Proverbs 22.9		2 Corinthians	9.7
Proverbs 25.21–2	LXX	Romans	12.20
Proverbs 26.11		2 Peter	2.22
Isaiah 1.9	LXX	Romans	9.29
Isaiah 5.1–2		Matthew	21.33
Isaiah 5.1–2		Mark	12.1
Isaiah 6.3		Revelation	4.8
Isaiah 6.9–10	LXX	Matthew	13.14–15
Isaiah 6.9–10	LXX	Mark	4.12
Isaiah 6.9–10	LXX	Acts	28.26–7
Isaiah 6.9	LXX	Luke	8.10
Isaiah 6.10	LXX	John	12.40
Isaiah 7.14	LXX	Matthew	1.23
Isaiah 8.8, 10	LXX	Matthew	1.23
Isaiah 8.12–13		1 Peter	3.14–15
Isaiah 8.14		Romans	9.33
Isaiah 8.14		1 Peter	2.8
Isaiah 8.17	LXX	Hebrews	2.13
Isaiah 8.18		Hebrews	2.13
Isaiah 9.1–2		Matthew	4.15–16
Isaiah 10.22–3	LXX	Romans	9.27–8
Isaiah 11.4		2 Thessalonians	2.8
Isaiah 11.5		Ephesians	6.14
Isaiah 11.10	LXX	Romans	15.12
Isaiah 14.13, 15		Matthew	11.23
Isaiah 14.13, 15		Luke	10.15
Isaiah 22.13		1 Corinthians	15.32
Isaiah 22.22		Revelation	3.7

INDEX OF OLD TESTAMENT QUOTATIONS

OT quotation	Version	NT passage	
Isaiah 24.17		Luke	21.35
Isaiah 25.8		1 Corinthians	15.54
Isaiah 27.9	LXX	Romans	11.27
Isaiah 28.11–12		1 Corinthians	14.21
Isaiah 28.16	LXX	Romans	9.33
Isaiah 28.16		Romans	10.11
Isaiah 28.16		1 Peter	2.6
Isaiah 29.10		Romans	11.8
Isaiah 29.13	LXX	Matthew	15.8–9
Isaiah 29.13		Mark	7.6–7
Isaiah 29.13		Colossians	2.22
Isaiah 29.14	LXX	1 Corinthians	1.19
Isaiah 29.16		Romans	9.20
Isaiah 35.3		Hebrews	12.12
Isaiah 35.5–6		Matthew	11.5
Isaiah 35.5–6		Luke	7.22
Isaiah 40.3–5	LXX	Luke	3.4–6
Isaiah 40.3	LXX	Matthew	3.3
Isaiah 40.3		Mark	1.3
Isaiah 40.3		John	1.23
Isaiah 40.6–8		1 Peter	1.24–5
Isaiah 40.13	LXX	Romans	11.34
Isaiah 40.13		1 Corinthians	2.16
Isaiah 41.8		James	2.23
Isaiah 42.1–3		Matthew	12.18–20
Isaiah 42.1		Matthew	3.17
Isaiah 42.1		Matthew	17.5
Isaiah 42.1		Mark	1.11
Isaiah 42.1		Luke	3.22
Isaiah 42.1		Luke	9.35
Isaiah 42.1		2 Peter	1.17
Isaiah 42.4	LXX	Matthew	12.21
Isaiah 43.20–1	LXX	1 Peter	2.9
Isaiah 45.9		Romans	9.20
Isaiah 45.21		Mark	12.32
Isaiah 45.23	LXX	Romans	14.11
Isaiah 45.23		Philippians	2.10–11
Isaiah 49.1		Galatians	1.15

INDEX OF OLD TESTAMENT QUOTATIONS

OT quotation	Version	NT passage	
Isaiah 49.6		Acts	13.47
Isaiah 49.8		2 Corinthians	6.2
Isaiah 49.18		Romans	14.11
Isaiah 52.5	LXX	Romans	2.24
Isaiah 52.7		Romans	10.15
Isaiah 52.7		Ephesians	6.15
Isaiah 52.11		2 Corinthians	6.17
Isaiah 52.15	LXX	Romans	15.21
Isaiah 53.1	LXX	John	12.38
Isaiah 53.1		Romans	10.16
Isaiah 53.4–6		1 Peter	2.24–5
Isaiah 53.4		Matthew	8.17
Isaiah 53.7–8	LXX	Acts	8.32–3
Isaiah 53.9		1 Peter	2.22
Isaiah 53.12		Luke	22.37
Isaiah 53.12		Hebrews	9.28
Isaiah 53.12		1 Peter	2.24
Isaiah 54.1		Galatians	4.27
Isaiah 54.13		John	6.45
Isaiah 55.3	LXX	Acts	13.34
Isaiah 56.7		Matthew	21.13
Isaiah 56.7		Mark	11.17
Isaiah 56.7		Luke	19.46
Isaiah 57.19		Ephesians	2.17
Isaiah 59.7–8		Romans	3.15–17
Isaiah 59.17		Ephesians	6.14, 17
Isaiah 59.17		1 Thessalonians	5.8
Isaiah 59.20–1	LXX	Romans	11.26–7
Isaiah 61.1–2	LXX	Luke	4.18–19
Isaiah 61.1		Matthew	11.5
Isaiah 61.1		Luke	7.22
Isaiah 62.11		Matthew	21.5
Isaiah 64.4		1 Corinthians	2.9
Isaiah 65.1–2	LXX	Romans	10.20–1
Isaiah 65.17		2 Peter	3.13
Isaiah 65.17		Revelation	21.2
Isaiah 66.1–2		Acts	7.49–50
Isaiah 66.1		Matthew	5.34–5

INDEX OF OLD TESTAMENT QUOTATIONS

OT quotation	Version	NT passage	
Isaiah 66.15		2 Thessalonians	1.8
Isaiah 66.24		Mark	9.48
Jeremiah 1.5		Galatians	1.15–16
Jeremiah 5.21		Mark	8.18
Jeremiah 7.11		Matthew	21.13
Jeremiah 7.11		Mark	11.17
Jeremiah 7.11		Luke	19.46
Jeremiah 9.24		1 Corinthians	1.31
Jeremiah 9.24		2 Corinthians	10.17
Jeremiah 16.16		Mark	1.17
Jeremiah 18.6		Romans	9.21
Jeremiah 22.5		Matthew	23.38
Jeremiah 22.5		Luke	13.35
Jeremiah 31.15		Matthew	2.18
Jeremiah 31.31–4		Hebrews	8.8–12
Jeremiah 31.33–4		Romans	11.27
Jeremiah 31.33–4		Hebrews	10.16–17
Ezekiel 12.2		Mark	8.18
Ezekiel 20.34, 41		2 Corinthians	6.17
Ezekiel 34.5		Matthew	9.36
Ezekiel 34.5		Mark	6.34
Ezekiel 37.27		2 Corinthians	6.16
Daniel 5.23		Revelation	9.20
Daniel 7.2–7		Revelation	13.1–2
Daniel 7.13		Matthew	24.30
Daniel 7.13		Matthew	26.64
Daniel 7.13		Mark	13.26
Daniel 7.13		Mark	14.62
Daniel 7.13		Luke	21.27
Daniel 7.13		Revelation	1.7
Daniel 7.21		Revelation	13.7
Daniel 7.25		Revelation	12.14

INDEX OF OLD TESTAMENT QUOTATIONS

OT quotation	Version	NT passage	
Daniel 11.31		Matthew	24.15
Daniel 11.31		Mark	13.14
Daniel 11.36		2 Thessalonians	2.4
Daniel 12.7		Revelation	12.14
Daniel 12.11		Matthew	24.15
Daniel 12.11		Mark	13.14
Hosea 1.10		Romans	9.26
Hosea 2.23		Romans	9.25
Hosea 2.23		1 Peter	2.10
Hosea 6.6		Matthew	9.13
Hosea 6.6		Matthew	12.7
Hosea 10.8		Luke	23.30
Hosea 10.8		Revelation	6.16
Hosea 11.1		Matthew	2.15
Hosea 13.14	LXX	1 Corinthians	15.55
Joel 2.28–32	LXX	Acts	2.17–21
Joel 2.32		Romans	10.13
Amos 5.25–7	LXX	Acts	7.42–3
Amos 9.11–12		Acts	15.16–17
Jonah 1.17		Matthew	12.40
Micah 5.2		Matthew	2.6
Micah 5.2		John	7.42
Micah 7.6		Matthew	10.35–6
Micah 7.6		Luke	12.53
Nahum 1.15		Ephesians	6.15

INDEX OF OLD TESTAMENT QUOTATIONS

OT quotation	Version	NT passage	
Habakkuk 1.5	LXX	Acts	13.41
Habakkuk 2.3–4	LXX	Hebrews	10.37–8
Habakkuk 2.4		Romans	1.17
Habakkuk 2.4		Galatians	3.11
Haggai 2.6	LXX	Hebrews	12.26
Zechariah 8.16		Ephesians	4.25
Zechariah 9.9		Matthew	21.5
Zechariah 9.9		John	12.15
Zechariah 10.2		Matthew	9.36
Zechariah 10.2		Mark	6.34
Zechariah 11.12–13		Matthew	27.9–10
Zechariah 11.12		Matthew	26.15
Zechariah 12.10		John	19.37
Zechariah 12.10		Revelation	1.7
Zechariah 13.7		Matthew	26.31
Zechariah 13.7		Mark	14.27
Malachi 1.2–3		Romans	9.13
Malachi 3.1		Matthew	11.10
Malachi 3.1		Mark	1.2
Malachi 3.1		Luke	1.76
Malachi 3.1		Luke	7.27
Malachi 4.5–6		Matthew	17.10–11
Malachi 4.5–6		Mark	9.11–12
Malachi 4.5–6		Luke	1.17

Index of New Testament Passages Containing Old Testament Quotations

NT passage	OT quotation	Version
Matthew 1.23	Isaiah 7.14	LXX
Matthew 1.23	Isaiah 8.8, 10	LXX
Matthew 2.6	Micah 5.2	
Matthew 2.15	Hosea 11.1	
Matthew 2.18	Jeremiah 31.15	
Matthew 3.3	Isaiah 40.3	LXX
Matthew 3.17	Isaiah 42.1	
Matthew 4.4	Deuteronomy 8.3	
Matthew 4.6	Psalm 91.11–12	
Matthew 4.7	Deuteronomy 6.16	
Matthew 4.10	Deuteronomy 6.13	
Matthew 4.15–16	Isaiah 9.1–2	
Matthew 5.5	Psalm 37.11	
Matthew 5.21	Exodus 20.13	
Matthew 5.21	Deuteronomy 5.17	
Matthew 5.27	Exodus 20.14	
Matthew 5.27	Deuteronomy 5.18	
Matthew 5.31	Deuteronomy 24.1	
Matthew 5.33	Leviticus 19.12	
Matthew 5.33	Numbers 30.2	
Matthew 5.34–5	Isaiah 66.1	
Matthew 5.35	Psalm 48.2	
Matthew 5.38	Exodus 21.24	
Matthew 5.38	Leviticus 24.20	
Matthew 5.38	Deuteronomy 19.21	
Matthew 5.43	Leviticus 19.18	
Matthew 8.17	Isaiah 53.4	

INDEX OF NEW TESTAMENT PASSAGES

NT passage	OT quotation		Version
Matthew 9.13	Hosea	6.6	
Matthew 9.36	Numbers	27.17	
Matthew 9.36	1 Kings	22.17	
Matthew 9.36	2 Chronicles	18.16	
Matthew 9.36	Ezekiel	34.5	
Matthew 9.36	Zechariah	10.2	
Matthew 10.35–6	Micah	7.6	
Matthew 11.5	Isaiah	35.5–6	
Matthew 11.5	Isaiah	61.1	
Matthew 11.10	Malachi	3.1	
Matthew 11.23	Isaiah	14.13, 15	
Matthew 12.7	Hosea	6.6	
Matthew 12.18–20	Isaiah	42.1–3	
Matthew 12.21	Isaiah	42.4	LXX
Matthew 12.40	Jonah	1.17	
Matthew 13.14–15	Isaiah	6.9–10	LXX
Matthew 13.35	Psalm	78.2	
Matthew 15.4	Exodus	20.12	
Matthew 15.4	Exodus	21.17	
Matthew 15.4	Deuteronomy	5.16	
Matthew 15.8–9	Isaiah	29.13	LXX
Matthew 17.5	Isaiah	42.1	
Matthew 17.10–11	Malachi	4.5–6	
Matthew 18.16	Deuteronomy	19.15	
Matthew 19.4	Genesis	1.27	
Matthew 19.4	Genesis	5.2	
Matthew 19.5	Genesis	2.24	
Matthew 19.7	Deuteronomy	24.1	
Matthew 19.18–19	Exodus	20.12–16	
Matthew 19.18–19	Deuteronomy	5.16–20	
Matthew 19.19	Leviticus	19.18	
Matthew 21.5	Isaiah	62.11	
Matthew 21.5	Zechariah	9.9	
Matthew 21.9	Psalm	118.25–6	
Matthew 21.13	Isaiah	56.7	
Matthew 21.13	Jeremiah	7.11	
Matthew 21.26	Psalm	8.3	LXX
Matthew 21.33	Isaiah	5.1–2	

INDEX OF NEW TESTAMENT PASSAGES

NT passage	OT quotation	Version
Matthew 21.42	Psalm 118.22–3	
Matthew 22.24	Deuteronomy 25.5	
Matthew 22.32	Exodus 3.6	
Matthew 22.32	Exodus 3.15	
Matthew 22.37	Deuteronomy 6.5	
Matthew 22.39	Leviticus 19.18	
Matthew 22.44	Psalm 110.1	
Matthew 23.38	Jeremiah 22.5	
Matthew 23.39	Psalm 118.26	
Matthew 24.15	Daniel 11.31	
Matthew 24.15	Daniel 12.11	
Matthew 24.30	Daniel 7.13	
Matthew 26.15	Zechariah 11.12	
Matthew 26.31	Zechariah 13.7	
Matthew 26.64	Psalm 110.1	
Matthew 26.64	Daniel 7.13	
Matthew 27.9–10	Zechariah 11.12–13	
Matthew 27.35	Psalm 22.18	
Matthew 27.39	Psalm 22.7	
Matthew 27.43	Psalm 22.8	
Matthew 27.46	Psalm 22.1	
Matthew 27.48	Psalm 69.21	
Mark 1.2	Malachi 3.1	
Mark 1.3	Isaiah 40.3	
Mark 1.11	Psalm 2.7	
Mark 1.11	Isaiah 42.1	
Mark 1.17	Jeremiah 16.16	
Mark 4.12	Isaiah 6.9–10	LXX
Mark 6.34	Numbers 27.17	
Mark 6.34	1 Kings 22.17	
Mark 6.34	2 Chronicles 18.16	
Mark 6.34	Ezekiel 34.5	
Mark 6.34	Zechariah 10.2	
Mark 7.6–7	Isaiah 29.13	
Mark 7.10	Exodus 20.12	
Mark 7.10	Exodus 21.17	

INDEX OF NEW TESTAMENT PASSAGES

NT passage	OT quotation	Version
Mark 7.10	Deuteronomy 5.16	
Mark 8.18	Jeremiah 5.21	
Mark 8.18	Ezekiel 12.2	
Mark 9.11–12	Malachi 4.5–6	
Mark 9.48	Isaiah 66.24	
Mark 9.49	Leviticus 2.13	
Mark 10.4	Deuteronomy 24.1, 3	
Mark 10.6	Genesis 1.27	
Mark 10.6	Genesis 5.2	
Mark 10.7–8	Genesis 2.24	
Mark 10.19	Exodus 20.12–16	
Mark 10.19	Deuteronomy 5.16–20	
Mark 11.9	Psalm 118.25–6	
Mark 11.17	Isaiah 56.7	
Mark 11.17	Jeremiah 7.11	
Mark 12.1	Isaiah 5.1–2	
Mark 12.10–11	Psalm 118.22–3	
Mark 12.19	Deuteronomy 25.5	
Mark 12.26	Exodus 3.6	
Mark 12.26	Exodus 3.15	
Mark 12.29–30	Deuteronomy 6.4–5	
Mark 12.31, 33	Leviticus 19.18	
Mark 12.32–3	Deuteronomy 6.4–5	
Mark 12.32	Deuteronomy 4.35	
Mark 12.32	Isaiah 45.21	
Mark 12.36	Psalm 110.1	
Mark 13.14	Daniel 11.31	
Mark 13.14	Daniel 12.11	
Mark 13.26	Daniel 7.13	
Mark 14.27	Zechariah 13.7	
Mark 14.62	Psalm 110.1	
Mark 14.62	Daniel 7.13	
Mark 15.24	Psalm 22.18	
Mark 15.29	Psalm 22.7	
Mark 15.34	Psalm 22.1	
Mark 15.36	Psalm 69.21	
Mark 16.19	Psalm 110.1	

INDEX OF NEW TESTAMENT PASSAGES

NT passage	OT quotation		Version
Luke 1.17	Malachi	4.5–6	
Luke 1.46–7	1 Samuel	2.1	
Luke 1.50	Psalm	103.17	
Luke 1.76	Malachi	3.1	
Luke 2.23	Exodus	13.2	
Luke 2.23	Exodus	13.12	
Luke 2.24	Leviticus	12.6–8	
Luke 2.32	Exodus	13.15	
Luke 2.52	1 Samuel	2.26	
Luke 3.4–6	Isaiah	40.3–5	LXX
Luke 3.22	Psalm	2.7	
Luke 3.22	Isaiah	42.1	
Luke 4.4	Deuteronomy	8.3	
Luke 4.8	Deuteronomy	6.13	
Luke 4.10–11	Psalm	91.11–12	
Luke 4.12	Deuteronomy	6.16	
Luke 4.18–19	Isaiah	61.1–2	LXX
Luke 7.22	Isaiah	35.5–6	
Luke 7.22	Isaiah	61.1	
Luke 7.27	Malachi	3.1	
Luke 8.10	Isaiah	6.9	LXX
Luke 9.35	Isaiah	42.1	
Luke 9.54	2 Kings	1.10, 12	
Luke 10.15	Isaiah	14.13, 15	
Luke 10.27	Leviticus	19.18	
Luke 10.27	Deuteronomy	6.5	
Luke 12.53	Micah	7.6	
Luke 13.35	Psalm	118.26	
Luke 13.35	Jeremiah	22.5	
Luke 18.20	Deuteronomy	5.16–20	
Luke 18.30	Exodus	20.12–16	
Luke 19.38	Psalm	118.26	
Luke 19.46	Isaiah	56.7	
Luke 19.46	Jeremiah	7.11	
Luke 20.17	Psalm	118.22–3	
Luke 20.28	Deuteronomy	25.5	
Luke 20.37	Exodus	3.6	
Luke 20.37	Exodus	3.15	

INDEX OF NEW TESTAMENT PASSAGES

NT passage		OT quotation		Version
Luke	20.42–3	Psalm	110.1	
Luke	21.27	Daniel	7.13	
Luke	21.35	Isaiah	24.17	
Luke	22.37	Isaiah	53.12	
Luke	22.69	Psalm	110.1	
Luke	23.30	Hosea	10.8	
Luke	23.34	Psalm	22.18	
Luke	23.35	Psalm	22.7	
Luke	23.46	Psalm	31.5	
John	1.23	Isaiah	40.3	
John	2.17	Psalm	69.9	
John	6.31	Exodus	16.4	
John	6.31	Psalm	78.24	
John	6.31	Nehemiah	9.15	
John	6.45	Isaiah	54.13	
John	7.42	Micah	5.2	
John	8.17	Deuteronomy	19.15	
John	10.34	Psalm	82.6	
John	12.13	Psalm	118.25–6	
John	12.15	Zechariah	9.9	
John	12.38	Isaiah	53.1	LXX
John	12.40	Isaiah	6.10	LXX
John	13.18	Psalm	41.9	
John	15.25	Psalm	35.19	
John	15.25	Psalm	69.4	
John	19.24	Psalm	22.18	
John	19.28–9	Psalm	69.21	
John	19.36	Exodus	12.46	
John	19.36	Numbers	9.12	
John	19.36	Psalm	34.20	
John	19.37	Zechariah	12.10	

INDEX OF NEW TESTAMENT PASSAGES

NT passage	OT quotation		Version
Acts 1.20	Psalm	69.25	
Acts 1.20	Psalm	109.8	
Acts 2.3	2 Samuel	7.12–13	
Acts 2.17–21	Joel	2.28–32	LXX
Acts 2.25–8	Psalm	16.8–11	LXX
Acts 2.30	Psalm	132.11	
Acts 2.31	Psalm	16.10	
Acts 2.34–5	Psalm	110.1	
Acts 3.13	Exodus	3.6	
Acts 3.13	Exodus	3.15	
Acts 3.22–3	Deuteronomy	18.15–19	
Acts 3.25	Genesis	22.18	
Acts 3.25	Genesis	26.4	
Acts 4.11	Psalm	118.22	
Acts 4.25–6	Psalm	2.1–2	LXX
Acts 7.3	Genesis	12.1	
Acts 7.3	Exodus	3.2	
Acts 7.5	Genesis	17.8	
Acts 7.5	Genesis	48.4	
Acts 7.6–7	Genesis	15.13–14	
Acts 7.7	Exodus	3.12	
Acts 7.18	Exodus	1.8	
Acts 7.23–9	Exodus	2.11–15	
Acts 7.27–8, 35	Exodus	2.14	
Acts 7.32–4	Exodus	3.5–10	
Acts 7.32	Exodus	3.6, 15	
Acts 7.37	Deuteronomy	18.15	
Acts 7.40	Exodus	32.1	
Acts 7.40	Exodus	32.23	
Acts 7.42–3	Amos	5.25–7	LXX
Acts 7.49–50	Isaiah	66.1–2	
Acts 8.32–3	Isaiah	53.7–8	LXX
Acts 13.22	1 Samuel	13.14	
Acts 13.33	Psalm	2.7	
Acts 13.34	Isaiah	55.3	LXX
Acts 13.35	Psalm	16.10	LXX
Acts 13.41	Habakkuk	1.5	LXX
Acts 13.47	Isaiah	49.6	

INDEX OF NEW TESTAMENT PASSAGES

NT passage		OT quotation		Version
Acts	15.16–17	Amos	9.11–12	
Acts	23.5	Exodus	22.28	
Acts	28.26–7	Isaiah	6.9–10	LXX
Romans	1.17	Habakkuk	2.4	
Romans	2.24	Isaiah	52.5	LXX
Romans	3.4	Psalm	51.4	LXX
Romans	3.10–12	Psalm	14.1–3	
Romans	3.10–12	Psalm	53.1–3	
Romans	3.13	Psalm	5.9	LXX
Romans	3.13	Psalm	140.3	LXX
Romans	3.14	Psalm	10.7	LXX
Romans	3.15–17	Isaiah	59.7–8	
Romans	3.18	Psalm	36.1	
Romans	3.20	Psalm	143.2	
Romans	4.3, 9, 22	Genesis	15.6	
Romans	4.7–8	Psalm	32.1–2	
Romans	4.17, 18	Genesis	17.5	
Romans	4.18	Genesis	15.5	
Romans	7.7	Exodus	20.17	
Romans	7.7	Deuteronomy	5.21	
Romans	8.36	Psalm	44.22	
Romans	9.7	Genesis	21.12	
Romans	9.9	Genesis	18.10	
Romans	9.9	Genesis	18.14	
Romans	9.12	Genesis	25.23	
Romans	9.13	Malachi	1.2–3	
Romans	9.15	Exodus	33.19	
Romans	9.17	Exodus	9.16	LXX
Romans	9.20	Isaiah	29.16	
Romans	9.20	Isaiah	45.9	
Romans	9.21	Jeremiah	18.6	
Romans	9.25	Hosea	2.23	
Romans	9.26	Hosea	1.10	
Romans	9.27–8	Isaiah	10.22–3	LXX
Romans	9.29	Isaiah	1.9	LXX
Romans	9.33	Isaiah	8.14	

INDEX OF NEW TESTAMENT PASSAGES

NT passage	OT quotation	Version
Romans 9.33	Isaiah 28.16	LXX
Romans 10.5	Leviticus 18.5	
Romans 10.6–8	Deuteronomy 30.12–14	
Romans 10.6	Deuteronomy 9.4	
Romans 10.11	Isaiah 28.16	
Romans 10.13	Joel 2.32	
Romans 10.15	Isaiah 52.7	
Romans 10.16	Isaiah 53.1	
Romans 10.18	Psalm 19.4	LXX
Romans 10.19	Deuteronomy 32.21	
Romans 10.20–1	Isaiah 65.1–2	LXX
Romans 11.2	Psalm 94.14	
Romans 11.3	1 Kings 19.10, 14	
Romans 11.4	1 Kings 19.18	
Romans 11.8	Deuteronomy 29.4	
Romans 11.8	Isaiah 29.10	
Romans 11.9–10	Psalm 69.22–3	LXX
Romans 11.26–7	Isaiah 59.20–1	LXX
Romans 11.27	Isaiah 27.9	LXX
Romans 11.27	Jeremiah 31.33–4	
Romans 11.34	Isaiah 40.13	LXX
Romans 11.35	Job 41.11	
Romans 12.19	Deuteronomy 32.35	
Romans 12.20	Proverbs 25.21–2	LXX
Romans 13.9	Exodus 20.13–15, 17	
Romans 13.9	Leviticus 19.18	
Romans 13.9	Deuteronomy 5.17–19, 21	
Romans 14.11	Isaiah 45.23	LXX
Romans 14.11	Isaiah 49.18	
Romans 15.3	Psalm 69.9	
Romans 15.9	2 Samuel 22.5	
Romans 15.9	Psalm 18.49	
Romans 15.10	Deuteronomy 32.43	
Romans 15.11	Psalm 117.1	
Romans 15.12	Isaiah 11.10	LXX
Romans 15.21	Isaiah 52.15	LXX

INDEX OF NEW TESTAMENT PASSAGES

NT passage		OT quotation		Version
1 Corinthians	1.19	Isaiah	29.14	LXX
1 Corinthians	1.31	Jeremiah	9.24	
1 Corinthians	2.9	Isaiah	64.4	
1 Corinthians	2.16	Isaiah	40.13	
1 Corinthians	3.19	Job	5.13	
1 Corinthians	3.20	Psalm	94.11	
1 Corinthians	5.13	Deuteronomy	17.7	LXX
1 Corinthians	5.13	Deuteronomy	19.19	
1 Corinthians	5.13	Deuteronomy	22.21, 24	
1 Corinthians	5.13	Deuteronomy	24.7	
1 Corinthians	6.16	Genesis	2.24	
1 Corinthians	9.9	Deuteronomy	25.4	
1 Corinthians	10.7	Exodus	32.6	
1 Corinthians	10.20	Deuteronomy	32.17	
1 Corinthians	10.22	Deuteronomy	32.21	
1 Corinthians	10.26	Psalm	24.1	
1 Corinthians	14.21	Isaiah	28.11–12	
1 Corinthians	15.25	Psalm	110.1	
1 Corinthians	15.27	Psalm	8.6	
1 Corinthians	15.32	Isaiah	22.13	
1 Corinthians	15.45	Genesis	2.7	
1 Corinthians	15.54	Isaiah	25.8	
1 Corinthians	15.55	Hosea	13.14	LXX
2 Corinthians	3.7	Exodus	34.30	
2 Corinthians	3.13	Exodus	34.33, 35	
2 Corinthians	3.16	Exodus	34.34	
2 Corinthians	4.13	Psalm	116.10	LXX
2 Corinthians	6.2	Isaiah	49.8	
2 Corinthians	6.16	Leviticus	26.12	
2 Corinthians	6.16	Ezekiel	37.27	
2 Corinthians	6.17	Isaiah	52.11	
2 Corinthians	6.17	Ezekiel	20.34, 41	
2 Corinthians	6.18	2 Samuel	7.8, 14	
2 Corinthians	8.15	Exodus	16.18	
2 Corinthians	8.21	Proverbs	3.4	
2 Corinthians	9.7	Proverbs	22.9	

INDEX OF NEW TESTAMENT PASSAGES

NT passage	OT quotation	Version
2 Corinthians 9.9	Psalm 112.9	
2 Corinthians 10.17	Jeremiah 9.24	
2 Corinthians 13.1	Deuteronomy 19.15	
Galatians 1.15–16	Jeremiah 1.5	
Galatians 1.15	Isaiah 49.1	
Galatians 3.6	Genesis 15.6	
Galatians 3.8	Genesis 12.3	
Galatians 3.8	Genesis 18.18	
Galatians 3.10	Deuteronomy 27.26	LXX
Galatians 3.11	Habakkuk 2.4	
Galatians 3.12	Leviticus 18.5	
Galatians 3.13	Deuteronomy 21.23	
Galatians 3.16	Genesis 12.7	
Galatians 4.27	Isaiah 54.1	
Galatians 4.30	Genesis 21.10	
Galatians 5.14	Leviticus 19.18	
Ephesians 1.2	Psalm 110.1	
Ephesians 1.22	Psalm 8.6	
Ephesians 2.17	Isaiah 57.19	
Ephesians 4.8	Psalm 68.18	
Ephesians 4.25	Zechariah 8.16	
Ephesians 4.26	Psalm 4.4	LXX
Ephesians 5.31	Genesis 2.24	
Ephesians 6.2–3	Exodus 20.12	
Ephesians 6.2–3	Deuteronomy 5.16	
Ephesians 6.14	Isaiah 11.5	
Ephesians 6.14, 17	Isaiah 59.17	
Ephesians 6.15	Isaiah 52.7	
Ephesians 6.15	Nahum 1.15	
Philippians 2.10–11	Isaiah 45.23	

INDEX OF NEW TESTAMENT PASSAGES

NT passage	OT quotation		Version
Colossians 2.22	Isaiah	29.13	
Colossians 3.1	Psalm	110.1	
1 Thessalonians 5.8	Isaiah	59.17	
2 Thessalonians 1.8	Isaiah	66.15	
2 Thessalonians 2.4	Daniel	11.36	
2 Thessalonians 2.8	Isaiah	11.4	
1 Timothy 5.18	Deuteronomy	25.4	
1 Timothy 5.19	Deuteronomy	19.15	
2 Timothy 2.19	Numbers	16.5	
Hebrews 1.3, 13	Psalm	110.1	
Hebrews 1.5	2 Samuel	7.14	
Hebrews 1.5	Psalm	2.7	
Hebrews 1.6	Deuteronomy	32.43	LXX
Hebrews 1.7	Psalm	104.4	LXX
Hebrews 1.8–9	Psalm	45.6–7	
Hebrews 1.10–12	Psalm	102.25–7	LXX
Hebrews 2.6–8	Psalm	8.4–6	LXX
Hebrews 2.12	Psalm	22.22	
Hebrews 2.13	Isaiah	8.17	LXX
Hebrews 2.13	Isaiah	8.18	
Hebrews 3.2, 5	Numbers	12.7	
Hebrews 3.7–11	Psalm	95.7–11	
Hebrews 3.15	Psalm	95.7–8	LXX
Hebrews 3.18	Psalm	95.11	
Hebrews 4.3, 5, 10	Psalm	95.11	
Hebrews 4.4	Genesis	2.2	
Hebrews 4.7	Psalm	95.7–8	
Hebrews 5.5	Psalm	2.7	

INDEX OF NEW TESTAMENT PASSAGES

NT passage		OT quotation		Version
Hebrews	5.6	Psalm	110.4	
Hebrews	6.13–14	Genesis	22.16–17	
Hebrews	7.1–2	Genesis	14.17–20	
Hebrews	7.17, 21	Psalm	110.4	
Hebrews	8.1	Psalm	110.1	
Hebrews	8.5	Exodus	25.40	
Hebrews	8.8–12	Jeremiah	31.31–4	
Hebrews	9.20	Exodus	24.8	
Hebrews	9.28	Isaiah	53.12	
Hebrews	10.5–7	Psalm	40.6–8	
Hebrews	10.12–13	Psalm	110.1	
Hebrews	10.16–17	Jeremiah	31.33–4	
Hebrews	10.28	Deuteronomy	17.6	
Hebrews	10.30	Deuteronomy	32.35	
Hebrews	10.30	Deuteronomy	32.36	
Hebrews	10.30	Psalm	135.14	
Hebrews	10.37–8	Habakkuk	2.3–4	LXX
Hebrews	11.5	Genesis	5.24	LXX
Hebrews	11.18	Genesis	21.12	
Hebrews	11.21	Genesis	47.31	LXX
Hebrews	12.2	Psalm	110.1	
Hebrews	12.5–6	Proverbs	3.11–12	LXX
Hebrews	12.12	Isaiah	35.3	
Hebrews	12.13	Proverbs	4.26	
Hebrews	12.15	Deuteronomy	29.18	
Hebrews	12.20	Exodus	19.12–13	
Hebrews	12.21	Deuteronomy	9.19	
Hebrews	12.26	Haggai	2.6	LXX
Hebrews	12.29	Deuteronomy	4.24	
Hebrews	13.5	Deuteronomy	31.6, 8	
Hebrews	13.5	Joshua	1.5	
Hebrews	13.6	Psalm	118.6	LXX
Hebrews	13.11	Leviticus	16.27	
James	2.8	Leviticus	19.18	
James	2.11	Exodus	20.13–14	
James	2.11	Deuteronomy	5.17–18	

INDEX OF NEW TESTAMENT PASSAGES

NT passage	OT quotation		Version
James 2.23	Genesis	15.6	
James 2.23	Isaiah	41.8	
James 4.6	Proverbs	3.34	LXX
James 5.11	Psalm	103.8	
1 Peter 1.16	Leviticus	11.44–5	
1 Peter 1.16	Leviticus	19.2	
1 Peter 1.24–5	Isaiah	40.6–8	
1 Peter 2.3	Psalm	34.8	
1 Peter 2.6	Isaiah	28.16	
1 Peter 2.7	Psalm	118.22	
1 Peter 2.8	Isaiah	8.14	
1 Peter 2.9	Exodus	19.5–6	LXX
1 Peter 2.9	Isaiah	43.20–1	LXX
1 Peter 2.10	Hosea	2.23	
1 Peter 2.22	Isaiah	53.9	
1 Peter 2.24–5	Isaiah	53.4–6	
1 Peter 2.24	Isaiah	53.12	
1 Peter 3.10–12	Psalm	34.12–16	
1 Peter 3.14–15	Isaiah	8.12–13	
1 Peter 4.8	Proverbs	10.12	
1 Peter 4.18	Proverbs	11.31	LXX
1 Peter 5.5	Proverbs	3.34	
2 Peter 1.17	Isaiah	42.1	
2 Peter 2.22	Proverbs	26.11	
2 Peter 3.8	Psalm	90.4	
2 Peter 3.13	Isaiah	65.17	
Revelation 1.7	Daniel	7.13	
Revelation 1.7	Zechariah	12.10	
Revelation 2.26–7	Psalm	2.8–9	
Revelation 3.7	Isaiah	22.22	
Revelation 3.19	Proverbs	3.12	
Revelation 4.8	Isaiah	6.3	

INDEX OF NEW TESTAMENT PASSAGES

NT passage	OT quotation		Version
Revelation 6.16	Hosea	10.8	
Revelation 9.20	Daniel	5.23	
Revelation 12.14	Daniel	7.25	
Revelation 12.14	Daniel	12.7	
Revelation 13.1–2	Daniel	7.2–7	
Revelation 13.7	Daniel	7.21	
Revelation 21.2	Isaiah	65.17	

Select Bibliography

Albl, M. C., *'And Scripture Cannot Be Broken': The Form and Function of the Early Christian Testimonia Collection* (NovTSup. 96). Leiden: Brill, 1999.

Beale, G. K., *The Book of Revelation: A Commentary on the Greek Text* (New International Greek Testament Commentary). Grand Rapids: Eerdmans; Carlisle: Paternoster Press, 1999.

Beale, G. K., *John's Use of the Old Testament in Revelation* (JSNTS 166). Sheffield: Sheffield Academic Press, 1999.

Bock, D. L., *Proclamation from Prophecy and Pattern: Lucan Old Testament Christology* (JSNTSup. 12). Sheffield: JSOT Press, 1987.

Brooke, G. J., *Exegesis at Qumran: 4QFlorilegium in its Jewish Context* (JSOTSup. 29). Sheffield: JSOT Press, 1985.

Brown, R. E., *The Birth of the Messiah: A Commentary on the Infancy Narratives in the Gospels of Matthew and Luke* (AB Reference Library). Revd edn. New York: Doubleday, 1993 (1st edn 1977).

Carson, D. A. and Williamson, H. G. M. (eds), *It Is Written: Scripture Citing Scripture. Essays in Honour of Barnabas Lindars.* Cambridge: Cambridge University Press, 1988.

Charlesworth, J. H. and Evans, C. A., *The Pseudepigrapha and Early Biblical Interpretation* (JSPSup. 14). Sheffield: JSOT Press, 1993.

Cope, O. L., *Matthew: A Scribe Trained for the Kingdom of Heaven* (CBQMS 5). Washington: Catholic Bible Association, 1976.

Dodd, C. H., *According to the Scriptures: The Sub-structure of New Testament Theology.* London: James Nisbet, 1952.

Evans, C. A. and Sanders, J. A. (eds), *Early Christian Interpretation of the Scriptures of Israel* (JSNTSup. 148). Sheffield: Sheffield Academic Press, 1997.

Evans, C. A. and Sanders, J. A. (eds), *Paul and the Scriptures of Israel* (JSNTSup. 83). Sheffield: JSOT Press, 1993.

Fawcett, T., *Hebrew Myth and Christian Gospel.* London: SCM Press, 1973.
France, R. T., *Jesus and the Old Testament: His Application of Old Testament Passages to Himself and His Mission.* London: Tyndale Press, 1971.
Freed, E. D., *Old Testament Quotations in the Gospel of John* (NovTSup. 11). Leiden: Brill, 1965.
Gamble, H. Y., *Books and Readers in the Early Church: A History of Early Christian Texts.* New Haven and London: Yale University Press, 1995.
Goulder, M. D., *Midrash and Lection in Matthew.* London: SPCK, 1974.
Gundry, R. H., *The Use of the Old Testament in St. Matthew's Gospel, with Special Reference to the Messianic Hope* (NovTSup. 18). 2nd edn. Leiden: Brill, 1975 (1st edn 1967).
Hanson, A. T., *The Living Utterances of God: The New Testament Exegesis of the Old.* London: Darton, Longman and Todd, 1983.
Hanson, A. T., *The Prophetic Gospel: A Study of John and the Old Testament.* Edinburgh: T & T Clark, 1991.
Hartman, L., *Prophecy Interpreted: The Formation of Some Jewish Apocalyptic Texts and of the Eschatological Discourse, Mark 13 par.* (ConBNT 1). Lund: Gleerup, 1966.
Hays, R. B., *Echoes of Scripture in the Letters of Paul.* New Haven: Yale University Press, 1989.
Juel, D., *Messianic Exegesis: Christological Interpretation of the Old Testament in Early Christianity.* Philadelphia: Fortress Press, 1988.
Knowles, M., *Jeremiah in Matthew's Gospel: The Rejected-Prophet Motif in Matthaean Redaction* (JSNTSup. 68). Sheffield: JSOT Press, 1993.
Koch, D. A., *Die Schrift als Zeuge des Evangeliums: Untersuchungen zur Verwendung und zum Verständnis der Schrift bei Paulus* (BHT 69). Tübingen: Mohr (Siebeck), 1986.
Koet, B. J., *Five Studies on Interpretation of Scripture in Luke-Acts* (SNTA 14). Leuven: Leuven University Press/Peeters, 1989.
Lim, T. H., *Holy Scripture in the Qumran Commentaries and Pauline Letters.* Oxford: Oxford University Press, 1997.
Lindars, B., *New Testament Apologetic: The Doctrinal Significance of the Old Testament Quotations.* London: SCM Press, 1961.
Longenecker, R. N., *Biblical Exegesis in the Apostolic Period.* Grand Rapids: Eerdmans, 1975.
Marcus, J., *The Way of the Lord: Christological Exegesis of the Old Testament in the Gospel of Mark* (Studies of the New Testament and its World). Edinburgh: T & T Clark, 1993; 1st publ. Louisville: Westminster/John Knox Press, 1992.

Menken, M. J. J., *Old Testament Quotations in the Fourth Gospel: Studies in Textual Form* (CBET 15). Kampen: Kok Pharos, 1996.

Moyise, S., 'The Language of the Old Testament in the Apocalypse', *JSNT* 76 (1999), pp. 97–113.

Moyise, S., *The Old Testament in the New.* London: Continuum, 2001.

Moyise, S. (ed.), *The Old Testament in the New Testament: Essays in Honour of J. L. North* (JSNTSup. 189). Sheffield: Sheffield Academic Press, 2000.

Müller, M., *The First Bible of the Church: A Plea for the Septuagint* (JSOTSup. 206/Copenhagen International Seminar 1). Sheffield: Sheffield Academic Press, 1996.

New, D. S., *Old Testament Quotations in the Synoptic Gospels and the Two-Document Hypothesis* (SBLSCS 37). Atlanta: Scholars Press, 1993.

Rutgers, L. V., van der Horst, P. W., Havelaar, F. W. and Teugels L. (eds), *The Use of Sacred Books in the Ancient World* (CBET 22). Leuven: Peeters, 1998.

Schuchard, B. G., *Scripture Within Scripture: The Interrelationship of Form and Function in the Explicit Old Testament Citations in the Gospel of John* (SBLDS 133). Atlanta: Scholars Press, 1992.

Skarsaune, O., *The Proof from Prophecy. A Study in Justin Martyr's Proof-Text Tradition: Text-Type, Provenance, Theological Profile* (NovTSup. 56). Leiden: Brill, 1987.

Soares Prabhu, G. M., *The Formula Quotations in the Infancy Narrative of Matthew: An Enquiry into the Tradition History of Mt. 1–2* (AnBib 63). Rome: Pontifical Biblical Institute Press, 1976.

Stanley, C. D., *Paul and the Language of Scripture: Citation Technique in the Pauline Epistles and Contemporary Literature* (SNTS Monograph 74). Cambridge: Cambridge University Press, 1992.

Stendahl, K., *The School of St. Matthew and Its Use of the Old Testament.* 2nd edn. Philadelphia: Fortress Press, 1968 (1st edn 1954).

Stone, M. E. and Chazon, E. G., *Biblical Perspectives: Early Use and Interpretation of the Bible in the Light of the Dead Sea Scrolls* (STDJ 28). Leiden: Brill, 1998.

Tuckett, C. M. (ed.), *The Scriptures in the Gospels* (BETL 131). Leuven: Peeters, 1997.

Index

Abel, murder of 72
allegory 9, 93n
Augustine of Hippo 13, 52–3, 68n

Balaam 19
biblical theology 1, 8
birth stories of Jesus 13–25

cleansing of temple 36–8
Corinthians' knowledge of scripture 76–8, 83–6, 91nn

Daniel 27–8
death of Jesus 37–8, 41–3, 50, 62, 76, 80–1, 87
Deuteronomic legislation 77–81, 92nn

'echoes' of Old Testament, criteria 53–62, 70, 81
Elijah 24
Eliot, T. S. 51–3, 90n
eschatological people of God 47, 58, 62, 63–6
Exodus 8, 9, 73, 76
Ezra, mourning 79

formula quotations
  introductory formulae 30, 82, 83, 92n
  Matthew's gospel 17–18

gematria (number symbolism) 15
genealogies 14–17
Gentile mission 63, 65, 75
gospel 4–5

Hannah's song 12, 21–2, 82, 84–6

intertextuality 28, 48–9, 88n, 89n, 93–4n
Isaiah, frequency of use by Paul 46–7, 66n, 67n

Jesus, etymology of name 20
John the Baptist 3, 21, 24, 30–1, 34–6
Joseph's dream 19
Josephus 14, 21
Justin Martyr 4, 5–6, 12, 130

kingdom of God 4–5

literacy standards 74, 89nn

Masoretic text (Hebrew) 32, 55, 69n, 82, 93n
metalepsis 52, 60, 70n
Moses 2, 19, 72

Noah's ark 9

Passover   24, 41–2, 43, 76, 80–1, 92n, 93n
Pharisees   2, 3, 59
Philo   85, 91n, 93n
proof-texts   5, 6, 7, 60

Qumran   2, 8, 11, 21, 22, 28, 47, 59, 69n, 73, 75, 88–9n

Revelation, book of   20, 26–8
righteous sufferer   38, 42–3, 45n

salvation, saviour   19–20, 58, 62, 65
scripture of early Christians   1–3, 5, 29, 48, 74–5, 88n, 130
Scrolls, practical limitations   74–5, 90nn

Septuagint
 style   21–2
 text   9, 32–3, 34, 36, 39, 42, 54–5, 82, 93n
 text revisions   32, 37, 45n, 68n
Shema   55, 69n
Suffering Servant (Isaiah)   6, 10, 12n, 31, 47, 49–51, 58–9, 60–1, 65, 67n, 68n, 69n, 70n, 75

typology   7, 64

vices, list of   78

Waste Land, The   51–3

www.ingramcontent.com/pod-product-compliance
Lightning Source LLC
Chambersburg PA
CBHW071502160426
43195CB00013B/2184